A History of
Dartford Harriers

Richard Drew   **Peter Field**   **Michael Holland**

Arthur Kimber   **Molly Titshall**

foreword by Steve Ovett OBE

Pen Press

First published in Great Britain

All paper used in the printing of this book has been made from wood grown
in managed, sustainable forests.

ISBN13: 978-1-78003-164-4

Printed and bound in the UK
Pen Press is an imprint of
Indepenpress Publishing Limited
25 Eastern Place
Brighton
BN2 1GJ

A catalogue record of this book is available from
the British Library

Cover design by Jacqueline Abromeit

Contents

Dedication

To all members of Dartford Harriers, past and present, together with all officials, coaches and others who have provided help and assistance to the club over all the years from 1922 until the present day.

Introduction

Peter Field had the concept of producing a book detailing the history of Dartford Harriers from its creation in 1922. After contacting a number of past and present members of the club, a group of five, including Peter, held an inaugural meeting at his house in late 2006. So the editorial committee was born and they set about the task of compiling all the information they could to enable this book to be produced and published.

Left to right:
Drew, Michael Holland, Arthur Kimber, Molly Titshall, Peter Field

Acknowledgements

Additional Material

Doris Batchelor: Scrapbook 1956/1957, two medals

Maureen Hodder née Conlan: Scrapbook, medal displays, framed relics

Alan and Joan Hutson: AGM documents, result sheets, newsletters (1947/1955) etc

Richard Drew: Interview Notes on Harry and Eva May and research relating to Bill Western

Arthur Head: Interview from club magazine

Joyce White (sister of Alf Bennett): letter re Alf Bennett's stage of Olympic Torch Relay

Peter Collins: Recollections on joining Dartford Harriers

Dave Nash and Mike Burgoyne: for specific help in compiling information on the Dartford Half Marathon

Various other members of the Diehards

Dartford Library

Gravesend Library

Bexley Local Studies and Archive Centre

Newspapers including:

    Kent Messenger (various editions)

    Gravesend and Dartford Reporter

    Kentish Times

    Other local and free newspapers

Photographs

Thanks to everyone who supplied photographic material for use in this book.

Statistics

Obtained from club records and other sources and compiled by Arthur Kimber.

The authors wish to express their thanks to Diane Holland for all her help in transferring the information to the computer and hosting their committee meetings and providing lunch. In addition, Melanie Lay for her assistance in guiding them through publication and marketing.

The editorial committee point out that gaps in information throughout this book are due, in part, to both loss and theft of club archive material. They have done their best but apologise for any errors and omissions. If any reader has any additional material that could be considered for use in any future revision of this book, please contact one of the authors.

Foreword

I was very pleased to be invited to write the foreword to this book on the history of Dartford Harriers. The club has a long history dating back to 1922 and counts among its members Olympian marathoner Sarah Rowell, European and Commonwealth Games marathoner Geoff Wightman and in 2010 celebrated Grace Clements's bronze medal in the Commonwealth Games heptathlon. It is local clubs like Dartford that are the backbone of British athletics and have been a vital part of the success we have enjoyed in the past.

I will always remember Dartford as the place where I ran the longest race in which I have ever competed, the Dartford Harriers' Half Marathon in 1977. I was expecting to compete in Edinburgh that weeken over the much shorter distance of 800 metres, but missed my flig I had not entered the half marathon, but as some of my Brighton Hove team mates were running I asked if I could take part and Referee Len Smith kindly gave me permission to run, but as entry I would not to qualify for the top prize, a very desirable p TV. More by luck than judgement I won the race and learned f experience that distance running is best left to those who enjo have never run another half or marathon since, although I ha up a few TVs along the way!

I understand that the club currently has about 200 me ing from youngsters to masters, not only competing in tr but also in road running and cross country. With the Ol coming to London in 2012 I sincerely hope that new m encouraged to join the club and that they and all existir go from strength to strength in the future.

I am very proud of our athletic heritage and the that have made it so, let's hope that our sport is e> the future.

I look forward to the publication and reading

Richar

Peter Field

Peter Field sadly died on 13th June 2010 and his presence and contributions to this book have been deeply missed by the remainder of the committee. It is certainly due in no small part to Peter's drive and determination that this project has been realised. The end of this introduction contains a tribute to Peter. This was compiled originally as an obituary to Peter by Arthur Kimber and it appeared in the magazine 'Masters Athletics'.

Richard Drew

Along with Peter Field, Richard Drew researched extensively the beginnings of Dartford Harriers and the pre-Second World War period where we have had no records to work from, other than newspaper reports and annual general meeting minutes. In addition, he has contributed several chapters. Matters were not helped by the loss of records and minutes some years ago in a car theft.

Richard joined Dartford Harriers in 1957 and was originally trained as a sprinter by Ray Springate and later by Makhan (Mark) Singh as a quarter-miler. During the winter months Richard enjoyed cross country running. Between 1978 and 1986 he ran seven marathons and numerous road races.

First elected to the club committee in October 1960, Richard took over as race secretary of the Dartford Harriers' Six-Stage Road Relay, from Peter Collins, in 1963 and continued in that position until the event ceased in 1987. He was elected a life member of Dartford Harriers in 1975.

In 1998 Richard was elected club chairman and finally left the club committee in November 2009 after 49 years' continuous service.

Arthur Kimber

Arthur took up athletics at the age of 11. He joined Dartford Harriers in 1975 and became a member of the committee in 1978. He was the senior men's team manager in the late 1970s and 1980s and has been the manager of the men's masters team since 1991. He has worked as an official (starter/marksman) since qualifying in 1983 and is the club's records compiler. He was elected a life member in 1997 and served as president from 2000 to 2005 and chairman from 2006 to 2009. He stepped down from the committee at the end of 2009. He has competed as a middle-distance runner throughout his time at the club and now competes in masters events. Since July 2009 he has been chairman of the British Masters Athletic Federation. He has written several of the chapters in this book.

Molly Titshall née Baker

Molly is a founder member and current leader of the Diehards group, comprising former athletes of the club. She was pivotal in obtaining details and reminiscences from these past members.

She joined the club aged 16 in the early 1950s, having enjoyed success in school sport and cycling but with no athletic experience. Initially Molly took to the long jump, in which event she represented Kent. She pioneered women's field events at the club, especially the shot put, holding at the time the club record. Molly served on the club committee as Ladies' Captain and press secretary.

Michael Holland

Michael was a second claim member at Dartford Harriers in the early 1960s, being first claim member to Polytechnic Harriers in London, where he lived at the time. Like Richard Drew, Michael was also coached in his early days by Makhan (Mark) Singh, a senior AAA coach in sprinting and middle distance. As a solicitor, Michael, and his firm Hatten Wyatt of Gravesend, carried out legal work on behalf of the club. This included the incorporation of Central Park Athletics Limited, as the legal entity, to enter into the formal lease as tenants thereby taking full responsibility for the new clubhouse and track, as required by Dartford Borough Council.

Michael became the 'secretary' to the editorial committee preparing agendas and minutes and organising the typing of the chapters.

Peter Field, 1931–2010

Peter died in June 2010 after a long battle with cancer. He was born in London and when he was a boy his family moved to Essex where he took up athletics and joined Southend AC. After national service in the RAF, Peter's work took him to Kent, where he joined Dartford Harriers in 1958.

He was one of the stalwarts of the club for over 50 years, holding a wide range of key positions: secretary, treasurer, chairman, president, starter, archivist and historian and he was made a life member to reward all his sterling work. He was a good chairman and committee man. With his extensive knowledge of athletics, he could put forward his well-informed views strongly, but at the same time he was an attentive listener to the views of others. Despite his ill health, he finally stepped down as president only in November 2009 and up until a few days before his death was still working on his contribution to the history of the club.

During these 50 years he was very active as an athlete. He was a totally committed and dedicated clubman, who would sprint, run middle distance, throw or jump to gain points. His main talent lay in hurdling, where he had a very successful record, particularly as a master athlete. Peter said that he was born just at the right time for masters athletics, as the movement was beginning to gain momentum when he turned 40 in 1971. (Coincidentally, the first veterans club in the UK, Veterans AC, was set up in 1931, the year of his birth.) He competed in the first masters international meeting in Cologne in 1972 and in the first WAVA Championships in Toronto in 1975. As the regional masters athletics clubs began to be founded in the late 1960s and 1970s, Peter enthusiastically became one of the earliest members of the SCVAC. Apart from a host of medals at regional and national levels, Peter won eleven individual medals at international championships, six gold, two silver and three bronze. His four best golds came in two European championships, in Malmö in 1996, where he won both hurdles races, and outstandingly in Poznan in 2006 as an M75, where he took the European record for 300m hurdles in a time of 55.81 and the British record with 17.18 for 80m hurdles.

Peter was well known, widely liked and respected by hundreds of master athletes, as shown by the large attendance at his funeral, and from the many apologies received from athletes who could not attend having already gone to Nyiregyhaza for the European Championships.

He leaves a wife, Elsie, brother Colin and sister Joy and many other family members and good friends, both in the athletics world and elsewhere. He will be missed very much by them all.

Arthur Kimber

Chapter One

Brief History

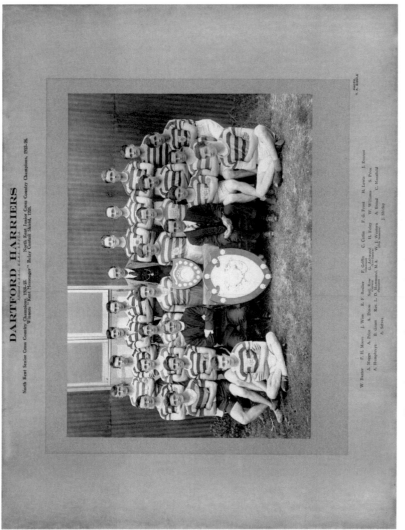

First known photograph of Dartford Harriers 1926

In April 1922 the Dartford Rugby Football Club was formed and registered to play by the Rugby Union governing body within the jurisdiction of the Kent County Rugby Union. They negotiated a part hire of the Glentworth Club ground, off Lowfield Street, to play matches. The nucleus of the new club comprised members of the Creek Athletic Rugby section, which at that time was very successful. Two XVs would play and represent the new club. It is on record that players would run cross country in these early days to keep fit for rugby and in the summer several members ran in athletics meetings. Bill Western was a one-time captain of the XV for DRFC. However, he gave up the game in 1923.

In 1922 club members took part in the Dartford Whit Monday Sports, the first club Track and Field Championships and the Kent Championships. In 1923 the club held its first Cross Country Championships from the Glentworth Club.

Up until 1926, the club used a grass track behind Dartford West Boys' and Girls' School. Then on 27th April 1926 the first AGM was held in the library, Church House, Lowfield Street. It is fairly certain that Bill Western and others, including Fred Griffin and Harry Dutton, felt confident enough to break away and run the now separate Dartford Harriers.

By 1930/31 the club headquarters and training was at the London Paper Mills sports ground, Princes Road, The Brent. The two outstanding athletes of the 1920s and 1930s were S G E Allnutt, a Southern Cross Country champion and Clarrie Dockerill, who twice won the Kent Cross Country Championship.

By 1938 the club quarters were Drill Hall, Lowfield Street, from where cross country runs were held in winter, while regular activities on the grass track in the Central Park Extension took place in the summer. This 'extension', an area somewhat larger than the current athletic arena, was added by bequest to the park.

Peter Collins remembers, 'When I joined the club in 1944 (at 14 years of age) with another chap from school who was a better sprinter, winter changing and cross country was from J and E Hall's sports ground. In those days there was no formal coaching, but the senior members were good at helping us with our training on an ad hoc basis. The older members worked at J and E Hall's and London Paper Mills. Harry May was very much in evidence filling the tin bath tubs with hot water. The first runners home in the cross country had clean water, but by the time the novices got back the water was pretty muddy.'

Soon after the Second World War, during which there was little activity, the club met and trained at Central Park in the summer and Hesketh Park in the winter. Until the late 1950s other activities, dinners/socials, dances, skating, shows, hikes, outings and ladies netball, seem to have been as prolific as running! These activities were organised mainly by Eva May (see chapter nine) and are remembered with great fondness by many of the Diehards (see chapter twelve).

For many years the track was marked out each season by Harry May with white lines on the undulating grass surface, while a small wooden hut in the corner of the park was the club headquarters. After at least ten years of discussion between successive council and Dartford Harriers' leaders, mainly Albert Taylor, Harry and Eva May, John Booker and Martin Mason, the cinder track was laid by Dartford Borough Council and opened in 1968. By that time the council had built a hut for the club to rent, twice the capacity of the original wooden one, together with the track. This had separate men's and ladies' changing rooms and a kitchen in between. As this was also better accommodation than the hut in Hesketh Park, it was soon used by the club in the winter as well.

During the 1960s Tony and Betty James were involved in many ways in the running of the club and in 1969 were elected as joint club presidents in recognition of their work.

Meanwhile, the club gained great popularity for its club Road Relay in each September (see chapter five). The races were held from 1960 to 1987. The Open Dartford Half Marathon was won by Steve Ovett when inaugurated in 1977 and is still held annually, being regarded as one of the club's best events. The cinder track lasted surprisingly well for around ten years, although maintenance had been minimal.

Then on 14th April 1984 a young South African, Zola Budd, was scheduled to run on the Central Park track as part of her attempt to gain British citizenship and a qualifying time to enable her to run at the Olympic Games in Los Angeles later that year. Zola won this 3000m track race in 9:02.6; a track record that survives to this day. The event was a comparatively small women's Southern League meeting, but it attracted world interest, being televised live in the United Kingdom and with a television crew from Australia. Central Park had unbelievable publicity and the cinder track was famously described as 'too dangerous to run on'.

In the meantime, the council needed the club hut as part of their new gardening nursery accommodation and the club moved to the Bowls Pavilion in September 1982, 200 yards away from the cinder track. Fortuitously this was helpful, as by that time the club needed larger premises to cope with the rising membership numbers. Patient collaboration with Dartford Borough Council since before 1984, under the leadership of club president, Nancy Wightman, culminated in the all-weather track opening in April 1987 by BBC commentator and coach, Ron Pickering. The club's contribution in both financial, around £30,000, and practical support, was most of the fixed equipment of the arena, and in improving the showers and building a toilet block.

Fatima Whitbread competed at Dartford in 1987 during the course of which she won the javelin competition with a throw of 72.40m, a stadium record which is unlikely to be beaten for a long time. This was Fatima's last competition in Britain before flying off to Rome where she won the gold medal in the World Championships with a throw of 76.64m.

The number of club members seems to have been consistently between 100 and 200 until 1975. That year a system of coaching, based on the Duke of Edinburgh's Five Star Award Scheme, was begun by a group led by Arthur Head. By 1987 the membership had increased to nearly 500. It is noticeable that some of this increase was coincident with the national enthusiasm of the time for road running and the arrival of the all-weather track. Amongst coaches who contributed considerably over many years were Peter Collins, Tony James (loyally supported in many aspects of club life by his wife, Betty), Jim Dray, Reg Wilson, and currently, Gary Capon and Alan and Rosemary Champion.

Because of the inadequacy of the pavilion, our supporters club agreed that their main aim would be to raise funds for a new pavilion. Application was made to the National Sports Council for a grant, which would depend on local council support for the project and to the Foundation for Sports and the Arts, which granted £75,000 dependent on the £33,000 the club and supporters had available.

In May 1993 vandals destroyed the bowls pavilion by fire. The firemen were still there as the club committee arrived for the monthly meeting! Within a few days, club volunteers with council help had made our old hut, now not used by the council in their nursery area, ready for our occupation. Also, we managed to obtain from National Power a disused portacabin to augment our now very inadequate accommodation.

By the end of 1993 the club had firm proposals for leasing, planning and building permission for a new clubhouse. It was necessary for the club to form a legal entity, namely Dartford Harriers Facilities Ltd (limited by guarantee), to enable the lease to be granted. The estimated cost was £260,000. Dartford Borough Council expected to be able to contribute the sum of £60,000. Fortuitously, the National Lottery Sports Fund had begun to function in 1994 and was able to award the club £90,000.

The first directors of Dartford Harriers Facilities Ltd were Linda Davidson, Peter Field and Alan Champion. Andrew Clarke agreed to take Linda's place in 1996 as the supporters club had effectively fulfilled their main objective, the necessary finance. Shortly before the completion of the clubhouse, the company name was changed to Central Park Athletics Ltd to distinguish it as a separate entity from Dartford Harriers. This was agreed between Dartford Borough Council and the club to be advisable.

The climax of seven frenetic years with a high workload for many members of the club was the opening of the new clubhouse on 1st September 1997 by Steve Backley, Olympic javelin medallist and a member of Cambridge Harriers. Many thanks are due to all the members of the club not named so far who worked so hard to achieve this, Mike Burgoyne, Audrey Dyett, Tony Farmer, Michael Holland, Paul Oakes, Derek Wightman and Geoff Wightman.

Since 1997 the clubhouse has been extended to create a room upstairs, which has been used for official meetings and social functions, such as quiz nights and discos. New floodlights have been installed and adjustable steeplechase barriers purchased to cater for all age groups, men and women.

Current Clubhouse of Dartford Harriers

The following is a record of the Life Members of Dartford Harriers since 1922:

Arthur	Board	1947
John	Boland	1960
John	Booker	1952
Alan	Bungay	2006
Mike	Burgoyne	1998
Gary	Capon	2005
Alan	Champion	1997
Rosemary	Champion	1997
Charlie	Childs	1966
Clarrie	Dockerill	1972
Jim	Dray	1989
Richard	Drew	1975

A W	Edmonds	1951
Peter	Field	1962
Dr G E	Foster	1951
Fred	Griffin	1947
Arthur	Head	1979
Alf	Hill	1984
Paul	Hills	2005
Eustace J	Hobbs	1952
Maureen	Hodder née Conlan	1969
Cllr Joe	Huggett	1957
Tony	James	1970
Betty	James	1970
Arthur	Kimber	1997
Martin	Mason	1973
Harry	May	1951
Eva	May	1954
Harry	Rogers	1973
Gill	Skellon	2006
Ian	Stanford	1998
Alf	Taylor	1966
Merv	Waterman	2006
Bill	Western	1930
Geoff	Wightman	1990
Cllr Nancy	Wightman	1991
Derek	Wightman	1997
Reg	Wilson	1995
John	Wright	2001
Jackie	Wright	2001

Chapter Two

Cross Country

The following should not be considered a comprehensive account as club records have been lost and most information has been acquired from local press accounts.

From its beginning in 1922, the Harriers quickly formed a cross country section. The first recorded competition was in March 1923 for the J C Beadle Five-Mile Cross Country cup, which was won in 1923 by F Turrell and for three years thereafter by Percy Row. By December 1924, Dartford Harriers' senior men's team was placed second in the Kent County Cross Country Championships held at Horton Kirby. It only took until 1928 for Dartford Harriers' senior team to win the Kent County Cross Country Championships, again held at Horton Kirby.

In November 1925, Dartford Harriers' team won the Mid and North Kent Division Five-Mile Cross Country Championships held at Littlebrook, Dartford. Dartford Harrier, S G E Allnutt, was the overall winner of that race.

In January 1926, Allnutt became Kent County champion, but unfortunately for Dartford Harriers, he emigrated to South Africa at the young age of 22.

The next Dartford Harriers star was to be Percy Row who, in 1928, won the Club Cross Country Championship for the fifth consecutive year and was a most valuable member of the club team.

Clarrie Dockerill was second in the 1929 North Kent Cross Country Championships and headed the winning team for Dartford Harriers. In 1931, he was Kent County Cross Country champion. In 1932, Clarrie probably had his best season, retaining his Kent Cross Country champion title, was placed second in the South of the Thames Cross Country Championship, sixth in the Southern Counties Cross Country Championship and second in the London Business Houses Cross Country Championship.

In 1930, the Dartford Harriers' team won the South of the Thames Juniors Cross Country Championship. Excellent runners for the club at this time also included G Ashwood, H T Foster, John Booker and Alf Bennett.

Harry Rogers was also successful in the mid 1930s. In 1936 the team won the cup at the Kent County Cross Country Championship for the second time in its history.

The Annual General Meeting of Dartford Harriers in 1939 decided that official club activities would cease due to the international crisis. However, some events did take place during the Second World War as several key members of the club were either too old to serve in the armed forces or were at home on war duties.

In 1946, after the end of the Second World War, Dartford Harriers' men's team was placed third in the Kent County Cross Country Championships. In 1947, the team won the North Kent Cross Country Championship from Hesketh Park with Martin Whenman coming first and Cliff Rosser second.

South of the Thames Junior Cross Country Championships was won by the club team in 1947 and in the same year Martin Whenman became Kent County Junior Cross Country champion.

At the Kent County Cross Country Championships in 1949, Charlie Childs finished fifth and in the team placings, Dartford Harriers' team came fourth.

In the 1950s, Dartford Harriers boasted a number of excellent distance and cross country runners including, in no particular order, Len Morris, Jim Kierans, Keith Batchelor, Ron Foreman, Frank and Alan Dyter and John Roberts.

Dennis Booker had a significant win in 1952, coming first in the South of the Thames Cross Country Championships and the club team was as always strongly represented by loyal clubmen, including John Cassell, Roy Le Mar and Ron Foreman.

Dartford Harriers' women's team placed third in the 1955 Kent Cross Country Championships at Maidstone with Doris Batchelor finishing in fourth place.

It can be seen, therefore, that although National Service had had a disastrous effect on most athletics clubs, Dartford Harriers still had the spirit, if not the ability, of pre-war days.

In 1960, Dartford Harriers came third in the Kent Cross Country Championships with John Morrison third in the individual placings. The next year, John Morrison was our star runner on the track and cross country.

The club had the honour in 1961 of staging the Southern Women's Cross Country Championship.

Malcolm Still became club cross country champion in 1964 and he was also an outstanding track and field athlete for Dartford Harriers.

The mid 1960s was the turn of Colin Ridley to shine, first as a junior and then as a senior athlete in both track and cross country events. He was ably supported by, among others, John Cassell and Keith Marshall.

In 1965, Malcolm Hodges won the Kent Youth Cross Country Championship over three miles.

In the chapter on outstanding athletes (chapter eleven), the reader will see that Maureen Hodder (née Conlan) was virtually unbeatable in cross country races. In 1963, 1964 and 1965, Dartford Harriers hosted several Kent County Men's and Women's Cross Country Championships.

Paul Hills joined the club in 1968 and, on his return from university, won his first of nine club cross country titles in 1971. In 1976, he won the North Kent Cross Country Championships, the same year in which Barry Nash won the club Ten-Mile Championship. The club hosted the Kent Cross Country Championship in 1977.

Gary Huckwell gained an England Junior International vest when he ran in Paris in the World Cross Country Championships in 1980, coming in twelfth. He was the second Englishman to finish.

Geoff Wightman won the Kent County Junior Cross Country title in both 1980 and 1981 and in the senior race, Kevin Steere was the winner in 1981. Gary Huckwell was the winner of the Kent Senior Cross Country Championship held at Maidstone in 1983. In 1986 Geoff Wightman was placed second in the Kent Senior Cross Country Championships, helping Dartford Harriers' team win the event for the third time in its history; the first being in 1928 and the second in 1936.

The same year saw Dartford Harriers Ladies help the Kent team win gold medals in the Southern Women's Cross Country Championship. Those ladies were Sarah Rowell, Anna Wittekind and Karen Dyett. This was an era of some outstanding athletes in the club including

David Powell, Ian Patten and Alan Camp.

Special mention should be made of Paul Hills, who for over 40 years has been a fine athlete and club official. For many years he has been the Men's Cross Country team manager, a job he continues to undertake to this day.

The Dartford Harriers' Men's Seven and a Half-Mile Cross Country Championship has taken place since 1927. The following athletes are those who have won this trophy twice or more:

Twice	Percy Row
	Martin Whenman
	John Morrison
	Malcolm Still
	Tony Durey
Three times	Keith Batchelor
	Andy Pickett
Four times	Colin Ridley
	Steve Wilson
	Clarrie Dockerill
	Ian Patten
	Charlie Childs
Six times	Geoff Wightman
Nine times	Paul Hills

Paul Hills – nine times winner of the Club Cross Country Championships

Chapter Three

Track and Field

In the early years, Dartford Harriers was mainly a cross country club, but some members did compete in track and field from as early as 1922, in the Dartford Whit Monday Sports and the Kent Championships. For training they used the grass track behind Dartford West Boys' and Girls' Schools and from 1930/31 the London Paper Mills' sports ground in Princes Road. By 1938 a grass track in Central Park was used, although it was only available in the summer, as it closed at dusk. The meetings were usually inter-club trophy matches or open events. Unfortunately, we have no record of track and field performances from the years before the Second World War.

The 1948 Olympic Games in London gave a boost to track and field in general. Club membership before the Second World War had been predominantly men, but after the war more women were joining the club, and they gained greater recognition from 1945 when a Women's Best Performance Trophy was presented for the first time following the Men's Best Performance Trophy in 1944.

Inter-club trophy meetings, such as the Dartford Gala and Ron Argent, open meetings and county championships continued to provide the main opportunities for competition until the 1970s. An important change in the track and field scene came in 1968 when the new cinder track replaced the grass one. From the 1950s until the completion of the all-weather track in 1987, Harry May unfailingly marked out the white lines on the track.

In the 1940s, 1950s, and the early 1960s, the best male athletes included Jim Kierans, Martin Whenman, Ray Springate, Alan Riddington, Alan Hutson, John Morrison and Malcolm Still. Jim won the Kent Mile Championship in 1947 in 4:28.0, Martin the three miles in a championship-best performance of 14:30.4 in 1951 and was Athlete of the Year in 1946 and 1948. Ray was the Athlete of the Year in 1949 and Kent champion at long jump from 1949 to 1954 inclusive and high jump in 1950 and 1951. Alan Riddington was Athlete of the Year in 1954. Two very notable performances came from John, who ran a mile in 4:07.9, worth 90.51% on the age-graded tables and Malcolm, a 1:51.0 880yds, 91.64%. John was Athlete of the Year in 1958 and Malcolm in 1959, 1960 and 1963.

The outstanding female athlete was Maureen Conlan, who was Athlete of the Year in five successive years, 1962–1966, a record still not surpassed. (Read more about Maureen in chapter eleven.) Other very good athletes included shot putter/long jumper Molly Baker, three times winner of the award in 1954, 1955, and 1959 (as Molly Titshall), and sprinter Rachel Grindell, twice winner in 1951 and 1952.

From the 1970s, the national and regional leagues began to be formed. The club has not yet reached the heights of promotion to the British League, but has joined the Men's Southern League, the Women's Southern and Kent Leagues, the National Junior League, the National Young Athletes League and the Veterans Southern League, finally providing competition for all age groups from under 13s to the oldest masters. (See chapter eight.)

The late 1970s and early 1980s were perhaps the high tide of track and field for the club, a time when many very talented athletes were members, with many of their club records still standing after 25–30 years. Geoff Wightman, male athlete of the 20th century, was without doubt the outstanding athlete of the period, and still holds 11 club track and field records. (See chapter ten.)

Other accomplished athletes included sprinters Ian Bishop and Paul Colwell, hurdlers John Giles and Steve Munday, middle-distance men Jon Grix, Bill Addison, Doug Ives, Keith Smith and Brian Law, jumper Roland Walker and thrower Malcolm Willden. Ian ran a 48.5 400m as an under 20, and Paul a very fast 10.8 for 100m as an under 17, age-graded percentage 94.90. Seniors John Giles ran a 15.2 110m hurdles and Steve Munday 400m hurdles in 54.82. As an under 20, Jon Grix ran 3:50.91 for 1500m, 90.42%, Bill Addison an indoor 800m in 1:55.7, while Keith Smith as an under 17, a very fast 800m in 1:54.2, 93.44%. Senior Roland Walker excelled at triple jump with 15:43. These fine athletes were backed up by many others not far below their standards. Looking at this wide range of talent, it is not surprising that the team reached the prestigious Southern League GRE Cup semi-final and the plate final of the GRE Cup in the Alexander stadium in Birmingham, in 1981.

Two interesting stories relate to this talented group.

At the end of the final match of the season, when the team finished top of the league, the athletes celebrated by organising an unique experience for the team manager, who had never run a steeplechase race, by throwing him into the water jump. One athlete enthusiastically took photographs of the incident and later gave copies to the team manager to remind him of the joyous occasion.

At another meeting Doug Ives appeared wearing a new and striking pair of shorts, that led his team mates to ask where he had bought them. Doug replied with a cross between a smile and a smirk on his face 'Miss Selfridge'.

The outstanding female athlete was middle-distance star Anna Wittekind. (Read more about Anna in chapter eleven.) Other very talented athletes were hurdler Donna Pert, and sprinters Ann Baldock and Hayley Clements. Donna's performances over 400m hurdles reached a very impressive high with a 61.54 clocking at age 16 and improved to 59.8 as a senior. The 61.54 is worth 97.28% and is the highest percentage score ever achieved by a Dartford Harrier, male or female. Ann Baldock, as an under 17, ran a 56.0 400m and gained international selection, and Hayley still holds a range of club records from 100m to 400m, including 11.86 for 100m as an under 15, 96.88%, and as an under 17, 200m in 23.9, 92.38%. She was selected for the European Junior Championships in Cottbus, East Germany in 1985 and won a 4 x 100m relay bronze medal in the British team that broke the national record with 44.78, finishing close behind winners East Germany, and silver medallists the Soviet Union. Donna was four times Athlete of the Year, Ann five times, Anna and Hayley twice each.

The running boom and the opening of the all-weather track in the late 1980s, led to a marked increase in the club's membership, which reached an all-time high of around 500. In the 1990s and into the 21st century, James Chatt was the outstanding male athlete. He still holds many club records ranging from 60m to 400m, including a 21.2 200m, worth 93.01% and a 46.82 400m, 92.46%. He represented Great Britain in the European Under-23 Championships in Amsterdam in 2001, running in the 4 x 400m relay, where he won gold, in a British team time of 3:05.25 and took silver in the 4 x 100m in 39.45.

He also travelled to South Korea as a member of the British team in the World Universities Championships. He was the club Athlete of the Year in 1998, 2001 and 2003. Other leading athletes were Kevin Marriner, 100m in 10.5, 93.90%, middle-distance men Jason Thompson, 800m in 1:50.9, 92.39%, and Rob Kettle, an indoor 800m in 1:50.82, 91.79%, and jumper Chris Davidson, who reached a 7.46m long jump and a 2.00m high jump.

In the early days of the new century, Max Hall and Gavin Comber stood out as promising youngsters. Max, a combined events athlete, achieved decathlon scores of 5357 as an under 17 and 6556 as an under 20, and he remains the club's best-ever pole vaulter with 4.10m. He was the club Athlete of the Year in 2005. Sprinter Gavin Comber ran a 200m in 21.55 as an under 20, 91.50%, and as an under 17 a more impressive 200m in 21.61, 94.35%. He was the Athlete of the Year in 2004.

The outstanding female athlete in the first decade of the century is undoubtedly Grace Clements. She holds more senior club records, eleven, and more all-age records, six, than anyone in the history of the club and was Athlete of the Year in 2006, 2007, 2008 and 2009. (Read more about Grace in chapter eleven.) Other very good athletes included sprinter Kelly Thomas who as an under 17 ran 100m in 11.77, 94.81%, and an even better indoor 60m in 7.67, 95.69%, and Kathryn Blackwood, an accomplished long and triple jumper, reaching 5.77m and 11.28m respectively. Hammer thrower Katy Lamb threw 53.13m for a score of 93.17%, the highest percentage ever recorded by a Dartford thrower and was Athlete of the Year in 1998 and 2001. Shot putter Julie Dunkley threw 14.36m as an under 20. Combined events athlete Chloe Hurley-Gale was Athlete of the Year in 2004, her highest percentage being 92.10% with an 11.20m triple jump as an under 17.

In the last few years, five very promising youngsters have joined the club. Foremost is Natalie Hickmott, who as an under 15 clocked 12.5 for 100m, 91.92%, combined events athlete Adam Chalk, who reached an octathlon score of 4836 as an under 17, with a 100m clocking of 11.28, 90.86%, and almost reached the magic 90% with four other performances over 89%. He was Athlete of the Year in 2009. Tim Billings ranks just behind Adam in the octathlon with 4806 points as an under 17. The Brown sisters Gemma and Sam, daughters of the talented Donna Pert, stand out. Gemma at discus winning a bronze medal in the English Schools Championships, and Sam with excellent club record performances at four hurdling events, 60m, 75m, 200m, and 300m. She has equalled one of her mother's club records but there are still four more to beat!

These five were part of the group of seven, a record number for the club, who were selected for the English Schools' Championships in 2009.

Statistics

To assist the reader, the following is an explanation of 'age grading'.

Age-graded tables enable comparisons to be made between athletic performances by males and females, at different events and at different ages, from eight to one hundred years. Using the standards in the tables, which correspond approximately to world records, and by carrying out a simple calculation, a performance can be given a percentage score.

Two examples, one for track and one for field, show how the system works.

Example one – Track
A man of 55 runs 100m in 13 seconds. The standard is 11.41 seconds. Divide the standard by the performance and multiply by 100 – 11.41/13.0 x 100 = 87.76%.

Example two – Field
A girl of 15 long jumps 4.90m. The standard is 5.77m. Divide the performance by the standard and multiply by 100 – 4.90/5.77 x 100 = 84.92%

The 100m is judged to be the better performance.

It is important to note that in track events the standard is divided by the performance, but in field events the performance is divided by the standard.

Performances over 80% are regarded as good and over 90% as very good.

The following are performances by Dartford Harriers club athletes, which produce an age-graded result of 90% or more.

Name	Event	Time or Distance	Age Group	Percentage
Adam Chalk	100m	11.28	Under 17	90.86%
James Chatt	60m	6.90	Senior	92.89%
	200m	21.2	Senior	93.01%
	400m	46.82	Senior	92.46%
Hayley Clements	100m	13.0	Under 13	92.07%
	100m	11.86	Under 15	96.88%
	200m	24.39	Under 15	94.05%
	100m	11.77	Under 17	94.81%
	200m	23.9	Under 17	93.30%
	200m	23.8	Under 20	91.51%
Paul Colwell	100m	10.8	Under 17	94.90%
Gavin Comber	100m	11.3	Under 15	93.89%
	200m	23.3	Under 15	90.42%
	60m	7.17	Under 17	93.30%
	200m	21.61	Under 17	94.35%
	200m	22.58	Under 17	90.30%
	200m	21.55	Under 20	91.50%
Jon Grix	1500m	3:50.91	Under 20	90.42%
Natalie Hickmott	100m	12.5	Under 15	91.92%
Chloe Hurley-Gale	Triple Jump	11.20	Under 17	92.10%
Rob Kettle	800m	1:52.7	Under 20	90.54%
	800m	1:50.82	Senior	91.79%

Katy Lamb	Hammer	53.13	Under 20	91.17%
Kevin Mariner	100m	10.5	Senior	93.90%
Donna Pert	400m hurdles	61.59	Under 17	97.20%
John Morrison	1 mile	4:07.9	Senior	90.51%
Keith Smith	800m	2:02.3	Under 15	90.94%
	800m	1:54.2	Under 17	93.44%
Malcolm Still	880 yds	1:51.0	Senior	91.64%
Kelly Thomas	60m	8.1	Under 15	93.70%
	60m	7.67	Under 17	95.69%
	100m	11.77	Under 17	94.81%
	60m	7.80	Under 20	91.02%
	100m	11.93	Under 20	91.11%
Jason Thompson	600m	1:19.8	Senior	90.33%
	800m	1:50.1	Senior	92.39%
	1000m	2:25.07	Senior	90.83%

Donna Pert – Highest age-graded score ever by a Dartford Harrier

James Chatt – holding one of his several 'Athlete of the Month' awards

Southern League Men's Team circa 1981
Back row, left to right: Doug Ives, Steve Munday, Jim Medes, Arthur Kimber, Alan Champion, Geoff Wightman, Mick O'Donoghue, Peter Field, Peter Champion, Graham Dray, Ian Bishop.
Front row, left to right: Anthony Marshall, Mike Hill, John Giles, Dean Powell, Jeff Champion, unknown, Gary Huckwell.

Chapter Four

Road Running

The Harriers were formed primarily as a cross country athletic club and soon included track and field members, so it is perhaps not surprising that road running did not figure much in their early activities. However, a few details survive of some members competing on the road.

On 2nd August 1922, Bill Western was second in the five-mile road race at Bexley Ex-Servicemen's Sports. In August 1925, Syd Row was second in a ten-mile road handicap race at Sevenoaks. In November 1929, Harry May ran in a five-mile road race at Rochester, although he ran as a member of J and E Halls Harriers, where he worked.

The Kent County AAA 20-Mile Championships were held in May 1939 from the Drill Hall, Lowfield Street, Dartford, with Bill Western as chief clerk of the course. George Gosling (a Dartford Harrier) was the fourth man home. These championships were also held at the same venue in February of 1943 and 1944.

Three Dartford Harriers are known to have taken part in the 'Olympic Torch Relay' from Dover to London in 1948. Alf Bennett carried the torch at Charing (near Ashford, Kent) but he was representing London Paper Mills. Jim Kierons carried the torch, probably in the Maidstone area, but he was representing the Kent Police (at the time he was a police inspector). Truly running as a Dartford Harrier was Alan Dyter who carried the torch from Riverhead (near Sevenoaks). It seems that only one athlete per club was chosen for each leg of this relay and Alf Bennett's torch is still held within his family. (See chapter thirteen for more details.)

In 1955, the club formed a new road team and ran in the 'Wigmore 15'. This team comprised Les Davis, Ron Foreman and Frank Dyter.

The next significant event was in September 1960 when Peter Collins was the first race secretary and organiser of the first Dartford Harriers' Six-Stage Road Relay. (See chapter five for more details.)

On 9th November 1963, Dartford Harriers Ladies won the Kent Women's AAA Three by One and a Half-Mile Road Relay Championship at Catford, south east London. The team comprised Janet Barrett, Janice Eyles and Maureen Hodder (née Conlan), who ran the fastest leg of the day.

By mid 1970s, distance road running became fashionable and in August 1977 the Dartford Harriers' Half Marathon was inaugurated with Dave Nash as first race director. This race was won by Steve Ovett. (See chapter six for more details.)

It appears from club records that in 1978, the club inaugurated a trophy for the marathon champion and the first winner was Barry Nash. By 1980 there were awards for club champion at ten miles road, half marathon, 20 miles and full marathon.

The 1980s probably saw the finest decade of road running within the club. The first London Marathon in 1981 saw several Harriers able to compete in this entry-restricted event. Many club records set at this time still stand today. Among them we find Roy Cozens's time of 7:04:00 for the London to Brighton Race (54 miles) and David Powell's 1:47:16 in the 1986 Worthing '20'. Other fine performances, unbeaten to date, came from Brian Buonvino, Mark Guichard, John Fitton and Peter Sargeant.

One of the highlights in the history of the club came in 1985 with Sarah Rowell coming 2nd in the ladies' race of the London Marathon and Dartford Harriers Ladies winning the team prize (Sarah Rowell, Sally Ann Hales and Elaine Payne). The same year Alan Monday set senior men records for the 100-mile and 24-hour races.

Ian Patten was the first Dartford Harrier male winner of the Dartford Half Marathon and was a Great Britain representative in the European Cup Marathon in 1987, held at Huy, Belgium.

In the women's category, Pat Halstead and Sheila Cousins also still hold club records from this era.

John Campbell, a New Zealander and top veteran runner, held the world best times in his age category at 10km, half marathon and full marathon.

Roger Friend then set club records at 10km and 25km in 1988 in the over-40 age group.

Into the 1990s and we find more long-standing records set by Tony Farmer and Bob Heywood. From the same era, Maureen Farmer still holds many records as does Audrey Dyett, who won the Flora 2000 London Marathon, women 55–59 age category, in 3:35:49.

Andrea Green was the first Dartford Harrier to win the ladies' section of the Dartford Half Marathon in 1999.

Finally in the 21st century, we find the second male Harrier to win the Dartford Half Marathon in Daniel Pyne. Consistently good times were also achieved by Tony Farmer and Tony Durey for the men and Audrey Dyett and Maureen Farmer for the women.

The road running section has been well structured for many years since the founding of the 'First Steps' section in 1991 by Alan and Rosemary Champion for beginners. Today this section is catered for under the guidance of Ken Pickett, Syd Goodwin, Maddy Crowe and Marcus Graves.

Chapter Five

Dartford Harriers' Annual Road Relay

In 1960, Peter Collins was the first race secretary for the Annual Six-Stage Road Relay. The original course was about three and a half miles per lap. Race headquarters was the old Downs School just in Green Street Green Road (off Princes Road).

Each lap started and finished outside the school and went down Green Street Green Road, right up and over Darenth Hill past Darenth Church (St Margaret's), right past the Chequers Pub, along Darenth Road to the traffic lights at Princes Road, right up Princes Road and right back into Green Street Green Road. This was long before the motorways were built around Dartford and provided a fairly safe and quiet course on the second Saturday every September. In those days, Saturday afternoon was comparatively traffic free, particularly along Darenth Road.

Harry and Eva May provided refreshments during the afternoon and Harry May helped mark the course with signs.

In 1962 Peter Collins left the area and the club; Richard Drew became the new race secretary. He had just joined the club committee and no one else was prepared to take on the post or the responsibility this entailed. Apart from the organisation, the main problem each year was buying six identical prizes for the first team and the second team. Very often shops had four of something but not six.

After several years, the race became too dangerous to stage on the original course as the traffic had increased considerably. The solution was to use the (nearly) traffic-free roads of the old Darenth Park and Southern Hospitals. Although each lap was considerably shorter (about two miles per lap), there was quite a climb up towards the end of each lap so it was reasonably testing. The other advantage was that, not only were the runners safe, but any spectators and young children were equally safe. After the race, Darenth Park Hospital provided sandwiches, cakes, tea, coffee or squash by way of refreshments. At the Downs School, Eva May always provided pre- and post-race refreshments.

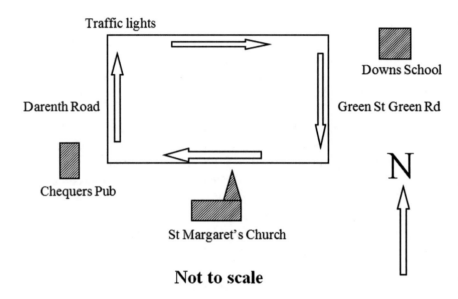

Not to scale

Some duties involving the race were:

    Advertise the race
    Arrange officials (timekeepers), marshals etc
    Arrange venue with KCC/Local Health Authority
    Mark course
    Deal with clubs' entries
    Organise prize presentation
    Arrange race results press release

Several years later the race venue was again changed for various reasons and became based at club headquarters in Central Park. The new course was to start and finish on the cinder track. Going out of the park via Cranford Road, Lowfield Street, left at the lights, up Princes Road to the left, down Brent Lane, left along Darenth Road, right at the lights, down Princes Road and into the park via Cranford Road again. This was about three miles per lap and still six times per team.

As headquarters was used, this cut out most of the expenses, although it never made a profit. It was considered a prestige event to promote the club. This was probably the best and most convenient course but eventually the traffic lights crossing at the junction with Princes Road became too dangerous and after several near accidents, a new venue had to be found.

The best that could be arranged was based at Dartford West Boys' School, Highfield Road. There was changing accommodation but no showers. The school canteen was useful for refreshments, prize presentation and shelter from the occasional bad weather on the day of the race. The course used part of the playing fields adjacent to the school, down the access road to the technical college, exit on to Miskin Road (opposite Rutland Place) into Shepherds Lane to the Princes Road traffic lights, left along Princess Road, left down Heath Lane, left at the roundabout, left into Summerhill Road, back into the school, up to the top end of the school fields and back down to the start/handover line. The distance was about 2.65 miles x six laps again.

In 1987, a new secretary agreed to take over from Richard Drew who had arranged the previous races. The new secretary had a contact that was going to sponsor the relay enough to stop the event making its annual loss. However, due to various circumstances, the new secretary never got the 1988 race off the ground and the event lapsed after almost 30 years.

This was unfortunate, not only because the event was a particularly important one for the club, but also that it was one of the oldest races to be held annually in the country, and because it was fairly low key, it was popular with the athletes who competed every year. We were always fortunate to have plenty of officials and pointsmen and so the event was well organised.

Dartford Harriers' Annual Road Relay Winners:

1960	Cambridge Harriers
1961	Blackheath Harriers
1962	Blackheath Harriers
1963	Blackheath Harriers
1964	Blackheath Harriers
1965	Cambridge Harriers
1966	Blackheath Harriers
1967	Blackheath Harriers
1968	Medway AC
1969	Invicta AC
1970	Thurrock AC
1971	Medway AC
1972	Thurrock AC
1973	London Irish AC
1974	Invicta AC
1975	Thurrock AC
1976	Invicta AC
1977	Invicta AC
1978	Invicta AC
1979	Cambridge Harriers
1980	Cambridge Harriers
1981	Invicta AC
1982	Invicta AC
1983	Invicta AC
1984	Invicta AC
1985	Invicta AC
1986	Cambridge Harriers
1987	Cambridge Harriers

Chapter Six

Dartford Harriers' Half Marathon

As previously mentioned, in the early 1970s road running became very popular and as Dartford Harriers had a serious road running section, the club felt there were not enough long-distance races within the county.

A small sub-committee of Harriers, including Dave Nash and Alan Monday, approached Tom Drady, an experienced organiser of road races, including the Harrow Marathon, for many years.

This led to the inaugural Dartford Harriers' Half Marathon being held on Saturday 20th August 1977. This event attracted a huge field, for that time, of nearly 200 competitors, including many British internationals. Those entering the event paid an entry fee of between £3 and £4. The sponsor was the Win Lighter Corporation of Japan, who provided prizes and generous funds for the expenses of staging the race.

The initial race headquarters was Madame Ostenburgh's College in Oakfield Lane, Wilmington, later part of Greenwich University. This venue had adequate car parking, showers, changing areas and a swimming pool.

Steve Ovett was a surprise late entry and to the consternation of many marathon runners, including Olympic marathon runner Barry Watson, Steve established a 16-second lead at the 10-mile stage. He cruised home a comfortable winner in 65:38 with a 21-second margin. Afterwards he claimed that he was just going to run a few miles of the race but found he was so comfortable and enjoying the experience, that he decided to go the whole distance. He did himself no harm as a fortnight later in the World Cup he set a British 1500m record of 3:34.5!

The sponsors were so pleased with the media coverage they received from Steve's win that they gave him a generous goodwill prize.

An interesting story from a later race is that the race secretary's sister-in-law was sitting in a traffic jam in the Dartford Tunnel on her way to assist at the event. To her surprise, and that of fellow motorists, a young lady ran past the stationary traffic heading in the same direction. It transpired that she had left her car for a passenger to drive as she felt she would have missed the start of the race. The young lady was Kath Binns, who went on to win the race for the ladies' section.

Over the years, the course had to be changed to different venues due to increasing traffic. As a result, comparative times are not relevant.

However, some notable performances have been achieved over the years; Keith Penny of Cambridge Harriers won in the years 1980 to 1986 inclusive and his wife Glynis, also a member of Cambridge Harriers, won a total of eight times in the ladies' section of the race.

Andrea Green, Dartford Harriers, won the ladies' section in the years 1999 to 2004 inclusive with the fastest time to date of 75:27 in 2000. Ian Patten and Daniel Pyne (both Dartford Harriers) were winners in 1987 and 2007 respectively.

The fastest time in the men's race on any of the three courses was recorded by Dave Chettle of Croydon Harriers and Australia when he won in 1979 in a time of 63:28.

The half marathon continues to be the main event in Dartford Harriers' calendar.

Winners (with their affiliations and times from the first staging of this event):

Men	Winner	Affiliation	TIME
1977	Steve OVETT	Brighton and Hove AC	64:38
1978	Keith PENNY	Cambridge Harriers	65:55
1979	Dave CHETTLE	Croydon Harriers and Australia	63:28

1980	Keith PENNY	Cambridge Harriers	67:24
1981	Keith PENNY	Cambridge Harriers	65:35
1982	Keith PENNY	Cambridge Harriers	67:23
1983	Keith PENNY	Cambridge Harriers	68:12
1984	Keith PENNY	Cambridge Harriers	68:35
1985	Keith PENNY	Cambridge Harriers	65:07
1986	Keith PENNY	Cambridge Harriers	67:28
1987	Ian PATTEN	Dartford Harriers	69:59
1988	Geoff JERWOOD	Herne Hill Harriers	69:04
1989	Gary ARTHEY	Blackheath Harriers	68:48

New one-lap course

1990	Gary ARTHEY	Blackheath Harriers	66:55
1991	Jeff MARTIN	The Army	69:45
1992	Geoff JERWOOD	Herne Hill Harriers	69:58
1993	Jonathan DAVY	Ipswich Jaffa	72:58
1994	Geoff JERWOOD	Herne Hill Harriers	70:50
1995	Amin KOIKAI	Ilford AC and Kenya	68:25

1996	Kassa TADESSE	Belgrave Harriers	70:50
1997	Scot McDONALD	Southampton AC	67:54
1998	Nick FRANCIS	Shaftesbury Barnet Harriers	68:48

Revised course

1999	Nick FRANCIS	Shaftesbury Barnet Harriers	69:21
2000	Nick FRANCIS	Shaftesbury Barnet Harriers	68:08
2001	John DOWNES	London Irish	68:45
2002	Simon BELL	Cambridge Harriers	75:20
2003	Andrew RAYNER	Blackheath and Bromley	74:40
2004	Steven WALDRON	UWIC	72:04
2005	Boukhemis BOUKHELIA	Thanet Road Runners	72:49
2006	Andrew GREEN	Dartford Road Runners	74:47
2007	Daniel PYNE	Dartford Harriers	80:33
2008	Peter TUCKER	Blackheath and Bromley	72:36
2009	Michael COLEMAN	Medway and Maidstone	69:33
2010	Dean LACY	Cambridge Harriers	72:23

Ladies	Winner	Affiliation	TIME
1977	Lynn BILLINGTON	Feltham AC	89:54
1978	Glynis PENNY	Cambridge Harriers	79:15
1979	Carol GOULD	Barnet Ladies	77:48
1980	Kath BINNS	Sale Harriers	77:24
1981	Kath BINNS	Sale Harriers	73:09
1982	Glynis PENNY	Cambridge Harriers	77:13
1983	Glynis PENNY	Cambridge Harriers	78:27
1984	Sally Ann HALES	unattached	77:06
1985	Sylvia KERAMBRUM	Wolves and Bilston	76:32
1986	Rosemary ELLIS	Hounslow AC	79:28
1987	Glynis PENNY	Cambridge Harriers	77:36
1988	Glynis PENNY	Cambridge Harriers	79:04
1989	Glynis PENNY	Cambridge Harriers	79:04

New one-lap course

1990	Glynis PENNY	Cambridge Harriers	80:19
1991	Glynis PENNY	Cambridge Harriers	82:52

Dartford Harriers' Half Marathon

1992	Heather HEASMAN	Invicta East Kent	80:42
1993	Alison FLETCHER	Cambridge Harriers	82:53
1994	Sue MARTIN	Medway AC	83:32
1995	Janice MOOREKITE	Invicta East Kent	80:46
1996	Birhan DAGNE	Essex Ladies and Ethiopia	80:31
1997	Birhan DAGNE	Essex Ladies and Ethiopia	80:48
1998	Janice MOOREKITE	Invicta East Kent	82:55

Revised course

1999	Andrea GREEN	Dartford Harriers	84:24
2000	Andrea GREEN	Dartford Harriers	75:27
2001	Andrea GREEN	Dartford Harriers	75:51
2002	Andrea GREEN	Dartford Harriers	75:53
2003	Andrea GREEN	Shaftesbury Harriers	78:39
2004	Andrea GREEN	Shaftesbury Harriers	79:59
2005	Kelly VENNUSE	unattached	85:15
2006	Kaeti MACKENZIE	Barnsley AC	88:02

2007	Tina OLDERSHAW	Paddockwood	84:30
2008	Tina OLDERSHAW	Paddockwood	83:17
2009	Lauren STEWART	Woodford Green/Essex Ladies	80:45
2010	June ALLEN	Springfield Striders	89:00

*Steve Ovett, the winner of the first Dartford Harriers'
Half Marathon in 1977*

Andrea Green of Dartford Harriers on all weather track circa 2000

Chapter Seven

Race Walking

This is not a comprehensive account as club records have been lost and most information has been acquired from the local newspaper reports.

The first mention of walking was in 1928 when the walking honorary secretary was Mr E G Lawrence.

In 1930, probably the first club championships, the One-Mile Walk was won by J Shirley who subsequently won this event again in 1931 and 1932.

Harry May, K Exeter and C M Martin were competitors in 1944 in a seven-mile walking race at Beckenham. In May of the same year, the Two-Mile Walk (Handicap) at Livingstone Hospital Sports was won by C M Martin.

Honorary secretaries were listed as F Whenman and A E Board in 1946. In March of that year, in the Kent Ten-Mile Walking Championships held at Bexley, C Murray was placed second and Harry May eleventh. In April, Margaret Smith was placed 13th out of 30 in the All England Women's Two and a Half-Mile Walking Championships in Birmingham.

By 1952 the Kent County 20-Mile Walking Championships were held in Central Park, Dartford. There then followed many years when walking was not so popular and also the club had no walking coaches.

From the mid-1990s, race walking coach and team manager, Mike Marshall, ran a successful walking group. Two of his group, Nicola Phillips and Natasha Fox, competed in the Junior England v Republic of Ireland match in Dublin in 2000. For a short time at the turn of the century, Sarah-Jane Cattermole was a member of the club and a successful walker. Mike was also instrumental in bringing the Race Walking Association National Championships to Central Park, Dartford in 2000, producing three national champions from the club. After Mike's retirement in 2006 race walking declined in popularity and today there is no race walking section.

Chapter Eight

Masters Athletics

There is often confusion about the use of the terms 'veterans' and 'masters'. When athletes over 40 were first recognised as a separate age category, the term 'veteran' was used in the UK, but 'masters' was used in the USA. The British governing body was at first the British Veterans Athletic Federation, BVAF, but it is now the BMAF. The European governing body is the EVAA, but the world body is the WMA. In this chapter the word 'masters' is used, but all organisations are referred to by their official names.

In the early years of the club, there was no such concept as masters athletics. The first club in the UK devoted to the idea, Veterans Athletic Club (VAC), formed in 1931, was a London-based club and attracted members for the south east, but we have no record of any early Dartford Harriers association with VAC. Most members of Dartford Harriers retired from active competition as their performances began to decline, either leaving the club or moving into coaching, officiating or administration. A few continued beyond 40, competing in senior track and field meetings or in open road races and cross country. Arthur Head and Les Davis were the most prominent, but there were no masters track and field meetings, except VAC meetings, or masters awards in road and cross country.

By the late 1960s and early 1970s, the masters movement, pushed forward particularly in the USA, was beginning to gain momentum. Regional clubs, in our area the Southern Counties Veterans Athletic Club (SCVAC) and a national organisation, the BVAF, were established, and they organised their own championships. The first international championship was held in Cologne in 1972 and was soon followed by a regular pattern of a European championship in the even-numbered years and a world championship in the odd-numbered. Peter Field was the first Harrier to join a regional club and compete in regional, national and international meetings, beginning with the Cologne meeting. He was followed in the late 1970s, when they reached qualifying age, by Kay Koppel, Arthur Kimber and Brian Barker.

A clarification on age qualification is useful here. Masters athletics began as a movement for men with a qualifying age of 40, but when women became involved, their qualifying age was set at 35. This anomaly was not finally rectified until 2003 when 35 applied to men and women.

In the late 1970s and 1980s, a high point for road running in the club, many road runners continued competing beyond 40; the outstanding among them were Brian Buonvino, Barry Nash and Roger Friend. Barry won the club Best Athlete of the Year award in 1976, 1977 and 1983. It was also the period when ultra-distance competition became quite popular in the club, with masters Alan Munday, John Fitton, Graham Ives and Peter Sargeant racing at distances up to 100k and 24-hour races. In the late 1990s and into the new century, Audrey Dyett stood out as the best female road runner, winning her age group, W55, in the London Marathon in 2000 with a fine 3:35:49.

At the beginning of the 1990s, the SCVAC track and field league began and a Dartford team joined the Kent division in 1991. This encouraged more senior athletes to continue competing and attracted into the club athletes already over 40, including parents of youngsters. In the later 1990s, a women's team entered the league and later a men's B team. Both men's and women's teams have had considerable success in reaching the regional final and placing well in it, especially in 2009, when both men and women reached the final. With the expansion of track and field and the popularity of road running, the masters now constitute the largest age group in the club.

Apart from the league, some masters have competed in regional and national championships, winning many medals, and beyond that in international championships, European and world.

Peter Field was the most successful, winning eleven individual international medals, six gold, two silver and three bronze. His greatest achievements came in the European Championships in Poznan, Poland, in 2006, where at age 75, he won the 300m hurdles in a European record of 55.81, 92.47% on age-graded tables, and the 80m hurdles in a British record of 17.18. Peter twice won the best athlete of the year award in 1973 and 2006.

Arthur Kimber has won four individual international medals, one silver and three bronze, with an age-graded performance of 89.44% for a bronze in the 800m in 2:34.57 at age 68 in the European Indoor Championships in Eskilstuna, Sweden, in 2005. Arthur twice won the best athlete of year award in 1978 and 2007.

Dave Kemp, although plagued by injury problems, has set eleven club records in recent years and also performed well in international championships

Pat Oakes is the only female to have won an individual international medal, a silver in the triple jump, 9.39m at age 50 in the European Championships in Malmö, Sweden, in 1996.

Kay Koppel, Pat Halstead, Anne Goad and Teresa Eades have all won many national medals and performed well in the international scene. Kay, as a W45, took fourth place in the European Championships in Brighton in 1984 with a 2:32.0 for the 800m; Pat, as a W50, was fifth in the 5000m with a time of 22:04.97 in Poznan, in the European Championships, and Anne was fifth in the pentathlon in the World Indoor Championships in Sindelfingen, Germany, in 2004. Anne also holds the W45 decathlon world record. Teresa, as a W45, reached sixth place in the high jump with 1.35m in the World Championships in San Sebastian, Spain, in 2005. Two promising newcomers recently into the masters scene are Cara Oliver and Kirstie Taylor, both of whom have performed well at national level.

Statistics

Performances over 90%, with age and percentage:

Brian Buonvino

5000m	15:09.8	43	90.84%
10k	31:55	45	90.54%
10 miles	51:04	44	92.62%
10 miles	51:52	45	91.87%

Arthur Kimber

800m	2:00.8	44	92.30%
800m	2:00.85	45	92.94%

800m	2:23.0	62	90.71%
1500m	4:05.4	42	90.59%
1500m	4:11.35	45	90.43%
3000m	8:50.5	44	90.99%
Peter Field			
60m	9.41	72	90.32%
300m hurdles	50.60	72	90.05%
300m hurdles	55.81	75	92.46%

Peter Field winning the 300m hurdles at European Championships in
Poznan in 2006 in a European record time
By kind permission of Tom Phillips Photos

Chapter Nine

Stalwarts of Dartford Harriers

All athletic clubs, Dartford Harriers being no exception, only function and survive because of the dedication and hard work of the few.

Four people who stand out in the history of the club are Bill Western, Harry and Eva May and Arthur Head.

William James Western (Bill)

The following is an account of Bill Western's association with Dartford Harriers, as revealed by press reports in the local newspaper and various records that have survived over the years. It is not by any means a comprehensive biography, as many of the club records have been lost.

William James Western was born in 1889 at Weston-super-Mare, Somerset. In 1909 and 1910, he won the Somerset Ten-Mile County Championship and in 1914 he is recorded as having come first in three one-mile open handicap races.

During World War I, he served in the Royal Army Service Corps. He moved to Dartford in the early 1920s and set up his own business as a sign writer. He is recorded as having won a three-quarter-mile race in Bromley, Kent and coming third in another mile race in Sidcup in 1921, whilst a member of Vickers Crayford Harriers.

As Dartford did not have an athletics club, he was determined to provide one, which he did.

In June 1922, he is listed as the contact for Dartford Rugby Football Club Athletic Team at 140 Dartford Road, Dartford. In August 1922, he was second in the five-mile open road race organised by the Bexley Ex-Servicemen's Sports.

By October 1922, he is in the list of the Dartford Rugby Football and Harriers Club, from which a team was to be chosen to run in a five-mile cross country at Erith AC. In November of that year, he was in the Dartford team selected to run at Chatham in the Mid and North Kent Five-Mile Cross Country Championship. He was also considered to run in the Kent County Cross Country Championship at Horton Kirby (seven miles). He also ran in the Kent County cross country championship at Horton Kirby (seven miles).

March 1924 saw Bill and H Dutton elected to the committee of the Kent County AAA Council. On 24th March of that year, H Dutton and Bill were judge and timekeeper respectively at the Mid and North Kent Area Three-Mile Junior Cross Country Championship at Dartford football ground.

The records show that by July 1924 Bill was living at 138 Dartford Road and in November of that year he and H Dutton organised the Mid and North Kent Division Kent County Athletic Cross Country Championship at Dartford (Littlebrook Farm).

Bill, H Dutton and F Griffin are listed as officials at the Kent County AAA Championships at Sittingbourne in June 1925. July 1925 saw Bill shown as the starter at the J and E Halls Sports.

Bill was clearly prepared to take on more administrative responsibility and by October 1925 he had been elected onto the course committee of the South of the Thames Cross Country Association and also onto the Kent AAA Cross Country Championship sub-committee.

The new Harriers club held its first General Meeting at Church House, Lowfield Street, Dartford in April 1926 instigated by Bill Western, who was still secretary of the club.

On 30th April 1930, Bill Western was elected the first ever Life Member of Dartford Harriers at their AGM.

Bill was not only the driving force of Dartford Harriers. In 1931 he became Kent County Cross Country team manager and on the County Executive Committee and later in November 1931, he was elected president of the South of the Thames Cross Country Association.

He was held in such respect by Dartford Harriers that the club members contributed enough money to purchase a gold hunter pocket watch, which was presented to Bill at the 1931 annual dinner and prize presentation evening.

It is fairly certain that he was instrumental in bringing the Kent Cross Country Championships to Dartford in the years 1931, 1932, 1933 and 1936, which would have involved organising the officials and other helpers.

Likewise in 1930, 1931 and 1936 he was responsible for the running of the South of the Thames Junior Cross Country Championships at Dartford.

In 1939 the inaugural Kent 20-Mile Road Running Championships were held in Central Park, Dartford – Bill being the clerk of the course. During the war, this event was also held at the same venue in 1943 and 1944. At this time Bill was Kent County AAA secretary and must have had a 'say' in deciding the venue.

At the London Olympic Games in 1948, Bill was honoured to be chosen as an official. He served as 'red sector' official for the six-mile section of the marathon course between Stanmore and Elstree War Memorial. His duties included control of time keepers, check recorders, pointsmen, feeding stations and transport.

Bill became President of Southern Counties Amateur Athletic Association in 1962 and he was also a vice-president of the national Amateur Athletic Association.

In the post-World War II years, Bill continued to organise very successful Dartford Harriers' dinner/dance/prize presentation evenings and always obtained very well-known sports personalities as guests. He could be relied upon to help the club in any capacity.

He was again voted in as club president in 1971/72 and in March 1972 presented prizes at the Dartford Harriers' buffet/dance/prize presentation evening.

From 1922 he served athletics in general, but Dartford Harriers in particular. He was the driving force that quickly made the club so strong, especially in cross country running.

Sadly in December 1972 Bill died and so closed a chapter in the history of Dartford Harriers. He had been the founder and a faithful servant of the club for 50 years. Could any club ask for more from one of its members?

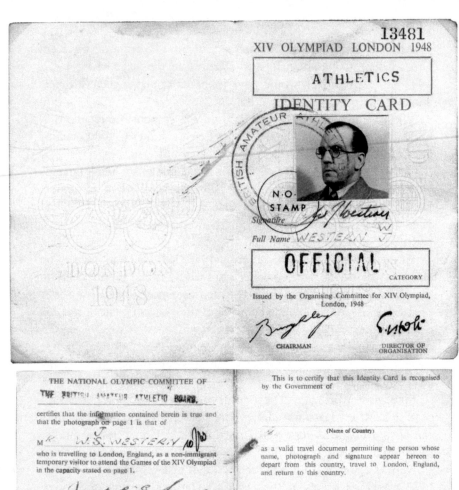

Bill Western's identity card for the 1948 London Olympics, 1948

Harry May

On the 19th March 1993, Dartford Harriers lost one of their oldest and certainly most loyal members.

Harry May joined the club in about 1925, and just missed being one of the founder members. In his early years he was a runner, but by the mid 1930s he became more interested in race walking.

If World War II had not broken out in 1939, he would have realised one of his great ambitions and competed in the annual London to Brighton (Stock Exchange as it was known) walk, which was, of course, cancelled that year. Even in his later years he spoke with regret at not being able to compete in this race.

During the war he was required to work in a reserved occupation, so he was able to continue living in Dartford and helping to keep the Harriers alive. In fact, all through his life, Harry worked hard to keep the club in existence.

After the war, the club continued and was now based in the far corner of Central Park. Harry helped with the running of the club, particularly on the practical side. He would mark out the grass track at the beginning of each season, repair the club headquarters and athletic equipment as necessary.

He regularly attended the club, opening the changing rooms and then locking up after training had finished.

Perhaps it would not be untrue to say that Dartford Harriers was his life.

During his later years, Harry took an active role in all aspects of the club, from serving on the general committee to carrying on with his practical help. Harry was a starter at a large number of meetings over the years and there was really no task that he would not undertake. He was always available to give advice or assistance when required.

Harry was fortunate to have in Eva, such an understanding and loyal wife. They were always together at the club for the various meetings and routine training nights, sharing the duties necessary to keep the club going.

People like Harry may come along once in a lifetime and Dartford Harriers owe a huge debt of gratitude to him for his selfless service to the club, spanning over 45 years.

He continues to be missed by all who were privileged to have known him.

Harry and Eva in July 1984

Eva May

On 22nd March 1996, Dartford Harriers lost another of its most loyal members with the death of Eva May, just three years after her husband, Harry.

Eva started her association with Dartford Harriers during the Second World War when she found herself helping Harry with the many tasks needed to keep the club going.

Whilst Harry was involved in marking out the grass track and looking after the athletic equipment, as well as many other chores, it soon became necessary for someone to make refreshments for the athletes after training or during competitions. As Eva was always at the Harriers with Harry, she gradually acquired this job and continued to provide this service well into her 80s.

Over the years, Eva's refreshments made a very reasonable profit which went to club funds.

When the club became based in Central Park, it had its own headquarters in a wooden building. The Mays always opened up, providing refreshments before cleaning and locking up at the end of the session.

In the winter months, Central Park was closed after dark so the members were able to use the old cricket pavilion at Hesketh Park on Tuesday and Thursday evenings. This also entailed opening up, lighting the gas boiler for warm showers and making tea on a portable gas ring. Often, on cold nights, no one would turn up for training but Harry and Eva were always there, just in case, not once in a while but twice a week, every week, come rain or shine, throughout 51 weeks of the year. They always allowed themselves one week's holiday in the early summer.

Eva and Harry gave over 45 years of selfless service to the club. They saw good and bad times but they were very dependable. Their attitude was always, 'What can I do for Dartford Harriers?'

Their love, devotion and dedication to the club should never be forgotten, and never will be by those privileged enough to have known them.

Arthur Head

Arthur Head has devoted all his spare time to Dartford Harriers and its membership since first becoming a member in 1947.

The following is Arthur's recollections of his time with the club as recalled for the club magazine some years ago:

'My interest in athletics was started by my father, who used to take me to see the AAA Championships and British Games meetings at the White City Stadium in London. This is where the great athletes of the world performed and they were a great inspiration to me. My school, like most schools in those days held one sports day a year and that was that. You might be picked for the District Sports, after which athletics were forgotten.

'After school days I went into the RAF, where I ran cross country at Aberystwyth in Wales as part of our strength training. We ran along the promenade and up Constitution Hill, an obstacle so formidable it had a funicular railway for normal mortals to get to the top; this was closed in the Second World War. Our PTI (physical training instructor) never looked back as he led us along the cliff top path, so he failed to see the heavy smokers, at least 50% of the total, dive into the bushes to eat blackberries until he came back on the return journey. They joined him one by one, so when he got back to the prom he had a full squad again.

'I joined Dartford Harriers in September 1947 at Hesketh Park, which was their winter headquarters. The subscription was seven shillings and six pence per year. In new money, 37.5p! Everything revolved around the cross country section. In fact, the cross country captain was called the club captain and he wielded much power, whilst the track captain took a back seat. This was in part the track athletes' fault, as once their summer season finished and rugby took over at Central Park for the winter season, they all went into hibernation, not to be seen again until the spring blossoms were emerging again.

'In contrast, the 'winter men', on finishing their strenuous efforts in the mud over the country, went straight into road relays for several weeks and then turned out for track training.

'At the beginning of the track season, Dartford Council would mark up one lap at Central Park with a white line to give the required 440 yards distance. Then Harry May would mark out all the other lanes with a spacer fixed to his line marker. Eva May was always there making the tea on her primus stove and listening to all the athletes' personal problems and checking that Harry had cleaned the toilets out properly!

'In those days there was no league structure and all matches were inter-club invitation meetings, some with a trophy at stake. These meeting were serious and hard fought, being reported in Athletes Weekly magazine. There was seldom any chance for hurdlers, steeplechasers or pole vaulters to take part in these meetings, except at County Championship level and above. The discus event usually took place without any sort of a cage around the circle. The high jumpers had no landing mats in those days and had to make the most of landing on a pile of sand!

'I remember that the final of the high jump in the 1948 Olympics in London had a massive 20 qualifiers and the gold medal was won by John Winter of Australia with a modest height of 1.98m, using the eastern cut-off style. It makes you realise what a service Flopper Fosbury did for high jumping with his revolutionary style and the help of foam rubber.

'The majority of javelins were fitted with a wooden shaft made of ash and I believe it still says in the rules that if a javelin breaks during a valid throw, it is not counted as an attempt.

'If, on the other hand, you wanted to become a qualified timekeeper, there were no cheap stop watches to be had in Argos as it did not exist in those days! A good wind-up watch would have set you back about five weeks' wages and then it had to be sent to the authorities to be certified before you could use it.

'There were always open handicap meetings that you could enter, but these became frustrating when you found out that an athlete who had beaten you by 40 yards in a mile race at a trophy meeting, turned up on his handicap mark about 30 yards in front of you. The maximum cost of the first prizes for these meeting was £12 and 10 shillings to preserve the amateur status of the athletes. Anyone caught selling their prizes or trophies was banned for life as a professional.

'I hope this gives a little idea of what life was like in athletics before subsidies, grants, insurance companies, agents, solicitors and politicians got their noses into the action and made our beautiful sport more complicated than it needs to be.

Lastly I would like to remind you that Dartford Harriers would not be here today without the tireless and totally voluntary work of Harry and Eva May, with over 45 years' service to the club. They were unique.'

Arthur has given invaluable help to countless club athletes during his time as a club coach and head coach, being regarded by all not just as a coach, but as a good friend. In recognition of his selfless devotion to the club and its athletes, Arthur received a glass trophy to honour his 60 years' membership of the club in 2007.

Arthur Head holding the 'Clubman of the Year' trophy 2008

Chapter Ten

Athletes of the 20th Century

Every year the Club Records and Best Performances committee chooses the Club Athletes of the Year. In 2000, it decided to select two athletes, one male and one female, as Athletes of the 20th century and voted unanimously, in both cases, for Geoff Wightman and Sarah Rowell.

Geoff Wightman

Geoff Wightman is the finest male athlete in the history of Dartford Harriers. He is the only male club member to date to have represented Great Britain in the European Championships and England in the Commonwealth Games.

He was born in 1960 and joined the club in 1973. He became interested in athletics when he ran in a cross country for the cubs in 1970. When he went to secondary school, Dartford Grammar, cross country was on the curriculum and as he ran well, his PE teacher suggested that he should join a club. He came to Dartford Harriers, a club with a membership then of nearly 100, with cross country as its main activity.

Geoff watched the 1972 Munich Olympics on television and saw Frank Shorter win the marathon. He says, 'I remember thinking, what a marvellous thing to win the Olympic Marathon. So I think that was always my dream from the age of 12, until the chance finally disappeared in 1992. And I got closer than most; in 1992 there were six of us with Olympic qualifying times and I was one of the three that missed out.'

As a boy in the club, Geoff continued with cross country and took up track running, becoming a very successful middle- and long-distance athlete. He still holds two under-20 club records. (See statistical section for details.)

In the early 1980s, Geoff was in the club track and field team when the club got into the Southern League GRE Cup semi-final and then to the GRE Plate final, held at Alexander Stadium, Birmingham, against much bigger clubs. Later he was in the cross country team that won the Kent Cross Country trophy, last won by Dartford Harriers 50 years before, and when the club placed 18th in the National Road Relays, beating the previous Kent top clubs, Invicta, Tonbridge and Blackheath.

Geoff's best performances came at his peak between 1986 and 1991, when he set 11 club records, all of which stand today.

An interesting story relates to his 5000m club record in Essen, Germany, in 1988. When he was preparing for the race, he realised to his dismay that he had brought two left-foot spikes. He looked like a non-starter. He then noticed Glen Grant, a Cambridge Harrier athlete whom he knew, and pointed out his predicament. Glen was not running in the same race as Geoff, and very fortunately took the same size shoe. Geoff borrowed Glen's spikes and ran 13:42.8 for an excellent club record, worth 94.60% on the age-related tables.

Geoff almost broke the four-minute mile barrier in 1988, with a time of 4:00.6. In the Berlin Marathon of 1991, he recorded a time of 2:13:17; this is his best age-graded score of 95.36%, and put him inside the Olympic qualifying time for 1992.

In 1990 in the European Championships in Split, then Yugoslavia, and in the Commonwealth Games in Auckland, New Zealand, Geoff took sixth and eighth places respectively in the marathon and was the only British finisher in both races. Geoff has vivid memories of both races and has spoken of how the pressure builds as the day approaches as he was conscious that it was not just another race, but, 'you're running for your country as well.'

The races were very different from typical marathons with only 40 starters in the Commonwealth Games and 63 in the European. In Auckland, Geoff was struggling with cramp in the final stages and was very relieved to cross the line. The race in Split began at 4:00pm in 27-degree heat and 60% humidity. The oppressive conditions produced relatively slow times; Gelindo Bordin winning in 2:14:02. Geoff left the stadium in last place, but he picked his way steadily through the field, even passing the Czech Karel David in the final run in on the track, covering the last 400m in about 70 seconds, for a final time of 2:18:01, less than four minutes behind Bordin.

Geoff believes that marathon success comes not from the overall volume of mileage. He rarely ran 100 miles a week. He says, 'I couldn't stand it. I used to get injuries or run down.' He emphasised a two and a half hour run on Sunday and intensive track workouts twice a week. Geoff retired in 1996, but later ran the Comrades Marathon (actually 56 miles) in South Africa. He has spent most of his working career in athletics. He has worked for Puma UK as a sports marketing manager, as UK Athletics Head of Road Running Policy and Support team, has written for Today's Runner and announced and commentated at meetings, including the London Marathon. He was, until recently, chief executive of Scottish Athletics but now is managing director of Run Britain, as part of UK Athletics.

Geoff is married to Susan (née Tooby), who ran for Great Britain in the Seoul Olympic Marathon in 1988. They have twin boys and a daughter.

Statistics

Geoff's best performances, with age-graded percentages, all still current club records:

Under-20 records	Mile	4:36.6	1978	83.68
	5000m	14:26.6	1979	90.34
Senior records	1500m	3:47.2	1988	91.41
	Mile	4:00.6	1988	93.26
	3000m	7:59.3	1986	93.66
	3000m indoors	8:08.42	1987	91.92
	2 miles	8:40.48	1982	93.42
	5000m	13:42.8	1988	94.60
	10000m	29:17.88	1989	92.06
	3000mSC	8:56.9	1986	89.78
	10k	29:23	1987	91.79
	10 miles	47:54	1987	93.24
	Half marathon	63:03	1986	94.68
	Marathon	2:13:17	1991	95.36

International championships

Commonwealth Games, Auckland	Marathon	8th	2:14:16	1990
European Championships, Split	Marathon	6th	2:18:01	1990

Split 1990 – Geoff Wightman.
Photo by kind permission of Mark Shearman

Sarah Rowell

Sarah Rowell is the finest female athlete in the history of Dartford Harriers. She is the only club member to have represented Great Britain in the Olympic Games.

She was born in 1962 and ran at school, but was at first mainly a hockey player, turning later to athletics as her main sport. She watched the first London Marathon in 1981 and thought it would be great to run one, and she ran London in 1982 and 1983.

Her coach, Cliff Temple, thought she should join a club and suggested Dartford. She joined in 1983, but being at college in Eastbourne, did not train at Dartford regularly. The track was cinders at that time and she said, 'If it had rained you put your wellies on as well as your spikes!'

Sarah's best performances came in the years 1983 to 1986. She won the World Student Games Marathon in 1983. In 1984 and 1985 she established six club records at distances ranging from five miles to marathon.

In the 1984 London Marathon, she finished third in 2:31:28. This performance qualified her for the Olympic Marathon in Los Angeles. The following year, 1985, in London she finished second in a new British record of 2:28:06, and as the first British woman to finish, led the club to the women's trophy supported by Sally-Ann Hales and Elaine Payne. This performance placed her a superb sixth on the all-time world list.

Like Geoff Wightman, Sarah pointed out that the Olympic Marathon had a small field compared to the usual big city races and with an early morning start there were few spectators. 'But you knew it was something special— At the end it was a totally different matter. I don't think you can describe running into a stadium of 100,000 people, who all started cheering—and you can see yourself on the screen at the far end; it's an incredible experience.'

Sarah finished 14th in 2:34:08.

She described her punishing training sessions in her build up to the marathons. 'I aimed to do around 80 miles one week and 100–110 the next and then back down to 80, alternating 80s to 100–110s. It was fairly standard, long run on a Sunday, couple of easy runs on a Monday. Tuesday would be a track session with a morning run, Wednesday would be 15 miles or so and maybe a second run. Thursday would again be morning run, theoretically 15 times one minute; minute easy, minute hard, but quite often it was a steady run because I would be tired. Friday would be an easy five-mile run and Saturday a sustained ten miles. One thing I found beneficial sometimes was doing a 15- or 20-mile run in the morning and a five-mile race in the afternoon.' Interviewer Arthur Kimber responded, 'Phew!'

Sarah thinks that her best athletic performance was winning the Seven Sisters Marathon, a very tough off-road race, in 1986. She won outright beating all the men and setting a new record in 2:49. Many experts think that this race is likely to add 30 minutes to your road time. Since then, only two men have beaten Sarah's time. The current record is 2:47. Unfortunately, the start of ongoing neural-related problems meant that Sarah was not able to run to the same standard on the road and had to withdraw from the Commonwealth Games later that year.

Since then, Sarah has moved to other tough challenges; fell and mountain running (at which she represented England, winning medals at the World Trophy), the Original Mountain Marathon (a two-day event mixing running, route choice navigation and self-sufficiency) and ultra challenges such as the Tour de Mont Blanc, a 100-mile punishing mountainous race round the perimeter.

Sarah has been involved in athletics in other ways, coaching and advising athletes and as chair of the UKA Mountain Running Advisory Group whose role includes selection of the world and European international mountain running teams.

She says that she cannot imagine life without athletics, as it has been part of her life for about 30 years. Her aim is to just keep enjoying it. 'I just like to lace up a pair of shoes and go out and come back having had a good run.'

Statistics

Sarah's best performances, with age-graded percentages, all still current club records.

Senior records

5 Miles	26:49	1984	no calculation possible
10 Km	33:34	1985	89.12
10 miles	53:44	1984	91.90
Half marathon	72:06	1984	91.26
20 miles	1:56:01	1985	no calculation possible
Marathon	2:28:06	1984	93.75

International championships

Olympic Games | Marathon | 14th | 2:34:08 | 1984
Los Angeles

Sarah Rowell – Second in the 1985 London Marathon
Photo by Mike Powell/Getty Images

Chapter Eleven

Other Outstanding Club Athletes

Grace Clements

Grace Clements is the first Dartford Harrier to win a medal in a major international championship, the bronze in the heptathlon at the 2010 Commonwealth Games in Delhi. Grace joined the club in 2000 and it soon became clear that she had the makings of a talented all-round athlete. She claimed to be bored unless she had several events to do in a competition! An important breakthrough came in 2001 when she was second in the heptathlon with 3621 points in the South East Schools' Championships and qualified for the English Schools, where she took sixth place with an improved 3818 points. In 2002 she won the South East Schools and gained her second English Schools selection, where she was fifth with 4286 points and helped Kent to win the team gold medal.

In 2002 she entered Cambridge University and in 2003 became athletics team captain, competing for Cambridge in the British Universities Championships and in the combined Oxford and Cambridge team in matches against American Universities; first against Penn and Cornell and then against Harvard and Yale. In the Harvard and Yale match she won the trophy for the outstanding female athlete of the match. In 2003 she was ranked 10th in the UK, 4268 points. In 2004 she was fourth in the under-23 rankings, 4513 points and in 2005 won the British Universities Championships heptathlon with 4903 points.

In 2006 when she competed in Woerden, Holland, her heptathlon score was 5256, which placed her fourth in the UK rankings for that year. In 2008 she competed in the British team in an international pentathlon, Great Britain v France, Spain and the Czech Republic, setting personal bests in all five events and took the silver medal with 4237 points.

After another international meeting in Szczecin, Poland, in 2009, she was again ranked fourth in the UK with 5740 points. When selected for the Commonwealth Games in 2010 she was ranked tenth in the Commonwealth, but exceeded all expectations to take the bronze medal with her best ever score of 5819 points. She said, 'I hoped not to come last.'

In the UK end-of-year rankings for 2010, Grace had moved up to third place.

Grace won the Club Athlete of the Year award in 2006, 2007, 2008 and 2009, holds six club under-20 records and an amazing 13 senior records, six of which are all-age records. As an athlete part way through her career, Grace is now looking forward to possible selection for the World Championships in South Korea in 2011 and the Olympic Games in London in 2012.

Statistics

Grace's best performances with age-graded percentages, all still current club records:

Under-20 records	300m	43.4	2002	79.17%
	100m hurdles	15.4	2003	83.11%
	High jump	1.70	2001	84.57%
	Pole vault	2.50	2002	59.10%
	Javelin	32.20	2002	40.12%
Senior records	60m hurdles	8.77	2008	87.86%
	100m hurdles	14.10	2008	86.59%
	High Jump	1.81	2008	86.60%
	Long jump	6.00	2010	79.78%
	Triple jump	12.41	2005	82.12%
	Javelin	44.32	2009	55.40%
	Shot	13.00	2008	60.60%

| Pentathlon | 4237 | 2008 | No calculation possible |
| Heptathlon | 5819 | 2010 | No calculation possible |

It is important to remember that Grace is a combined events athlete and not a specialist in any single event, but still manages to score highly in many events.

International championships

Meeting	Event	Place	Score	Year
Home Counties International, Stoke	Heptathlon	3rd	5366	2007
GB v France, Spain, Czech Republic, Sheffield	Pentathlon	2nd	4237	2008
Europa Cup (eight European Countries), Hengelo	Heptathlon	16th	5682	2008
GB v France, Spain, Czech Republic, Zaragoza	Pentathlon	11th	3886	2009
Europa Cup, Szczecin	Heptathlon	13th	5740	2009
GB v France, Spain, Czech Republic, Holland	Pentathlon	8th	4046	2010
Europa Cup, Tallinn	Heptathlon	9th	5755	2010
Commonwealth Games, Delhi	Heptathlon	3rd	5819	2010

Grace with Bronze medal, Delhi 2010
Photo by Michael Steele/Getty Images

Grace on lap of honour after coming third in Delhi 2010.
Photo by Mark Dadswell/Getty Images

Maureen Hodder (née Conlan)

Maureen Hodder was the first Dartford Harrier to gain an international vest. She joined the club in 1959 and she describes those early days, 'Club facilities comprised a wooden hut with a central partition, separating male and female changing areas, minimal lighting, with washing from an enamel bowl of cold water, provided by the ever-reliable Eva May, who always had tea ready for us. The track was grass, open to the public, complete with bikes and dogs.'

As a senior in the 1960s and a veteran in the1970s, Maureen was an active athlete and officer of the club, a timekeeper and a member of the Kent AAA as cross country secretary, and Kent Schools' committees.

She became a life member before emigrating to Ireland in 1982.

When evaluating Maureen's performances, it is important to re-alise the she competed on grass and cinder tracks, not on the faster all-weather surfaces that we are familiar with today and she raced at imperial distances that are not recognised, apart from the mile, for record purposes today.

Her international vest was gained competing for Ireland in the Home International Cross Country (England v Scotland, Wales and Ireland) in 1967. Maureen finished in 13th place and helped Ireland to take the second team place. On the track, her best performances were 59.02 for 440 yards, 880 yards in 2:12.03 and the mile in 5:02.00. In 1964 she won the Southern Cross Country Championship leading all the way and in 1966 was placed second in the National Cross Country Championship, where 79 finished.

On the track, her time of 2:12.03 in the National Championships in 1966 placed her 16th in the national rankings, and her mile in 5:02.00 in 1965 placed her fourth in the national rankings, behind leader Joyce Smith's 4:54.0.

Her indoor mile at Cosford in 1967 in 5:31.09, gave her eighth place in the national rankings. Maureen's performances made her five times winner in 1962, 1963, 1964, 1965, and 1966, of the club trophy for the Best Female Athlete of the Year, a record still unbeaten. No woman has yet won six.

Maureen still comes to the UK occasionally and visited Dartford in 2006 to see old friends and donate, very generously, her athletics memorabilia and medals to the club. She also presented the club with a new trophy for the Most Dedicated Athlete of the Year.

Statistics

Maureen's best performances, with age-related percentages:

440 yards	59.02	1966	81.61
880 yards	2:12.03	1966	85.95
Mile	5:02.00	1965	82.44

International Championship

Home Countries XC International, Barry	13th	16.22	1967

Maureen Hodder (née Conlan) leading the finalists in the women's one mile at the AAA Championships in the White City Stadium, 4th July 1965, where she finished fourth.

Anna Wittekind

Anna Wittekind is one of the finest athletes ever to wear a Dartford Harriers vest. Joining the club in the late 1970s and competing through the 1980s she set, and still holds, two under-15, one under-17 and eight senior club records, plus a share of a senior relay record. Her 800m time of 2:06.5 and her 1500m time of 4:18.07, both set in 1983, are club all age records. She won the trophy for the Best Female Athlete in 1979 and 1988.

Anna won three English Schools' titles; the 800m in 1982 in 2:10.3, and again in 1983, when she beat Diane Edwards (Modahl) into second place, both girls clocking 2:10.1, and the cross country title in 1983.

Athletics Weekly reported on the 1983 800m race that, 'Anna Wittekind's title took some defending. Diane Edwards looked through the qualifying rounds the girl best equipped to push Anna, and so it proved. With 200 metres left, it was either girl's race, but Anna wound up the pace coming off the final bend, stole a metre with 50 left, and held on gamely to win.' The photo finish of the race, below, was published in Diane's autobiography.

After one kilometre in the cross country race in 1983 Anna shared the lead with Carol Haigh. Carol made a break 1200 metres from home that looked decisive, but the gap was never more than eight metres, and Anna pulled it back economically, passed Carol and won by a clear nine-second margin.

Anna was selected for England in the 1500m for the Junior Women's Home Countries International versus Scotland, Wales and Ireland in 1982 and finished fourth in 4:35.6. In 1988 she was selected for the British team in the match against Czechoslovakia, Bulgaria and Greece in Prague and finished fifth in the 3000m in 9:24.0, and sixth in the 1500m in 4:27.0.

In 1988 she ran for England in the Home Countries International, finishing third behind winner Zola Budd. In 1983 she was a travelling reserve in the British team for the World Cross Country Championships.

Persistent injury problems affected Anna and she retired from serious competition, but still runs to keep fit. She has maintained her interest in the club and in 2009 was the guest of honour, presenting the trophies and inspiring our athletes, at our annual presentation evening.

Statistics

Anna's best performances, with age-graded percentages, all still current club records:

Under-15 records	150m	19.9	1979	no calculation possible
	800m	2:17.1	1979	88.11
Under-17 record	1500m	4:38.3	1982	85.12
Senior records	600m	1:28.1	1983	90.73
	800m	2:06.5	1983	89.23
	1000m	2:51.7	1982	85.16
	1500m	4:18.07	1983	89.30
	1500m indoor	4:27.22	1984	86.24
	Mile	4:50.0	1988	85.85
	3000m	9:19.11	1988	89.07
	3000m indoor	9:28.6	1984	87.58

International championships

Junior Home Countries International, Edinburgh	1500m	4th	4:36.6	1982
Senior International, Prague	1500m	6th	4:27.0	1988
	3000m	5th	9:24.0	
Senior Home Countries Cross Country International, Aldershot		3rd	18:40	1988

*Anna Wittekind just beats Diane Edwards to win the
English Schools' 800m final, 1983*

Chapter Twelve

Diehards
(former Dartford Harrier members)

Rachel and Alan Riddington met when they were active members of Dartford Harriers in the 1950s. They subsequently married and had four children.

As Rachel's 60th birthday approached in 1998, Alan decided, by way of a radio appeal, to try and contact some of her former team mates at Dartford Harriers. He successfully traced Joyce Marchant (née Wiseman) and Molly Titshall (née Baker) who joined the celebrations.

During that afternoon, the idea emerged to see if more friends from their Dartford Harriers athletic era could be traced. An initial meeting was held of people who had been approached to see if they would be interested in helping to organise a full reunion group.

The first reunion was arranged and held at Dartford Harriers' Central Park Pavilion in September 1999. The event was well attended by former members with displays of photographs and memorabilia from 'the old days'. With a buffet supper and a fundraising raffle, the evening was a rewarding success and all in attendance agreed to make this an annual event.

There has been a reunion every year since 1999 and other former club athletes have been 'found' and joined in and renewed old friendships.

Although there is an open invitation to friends from any era, most of those who have attended are over 50 years old. The group would like to locate more former members so they can also join in these convivial evenings of reminiscing.

A buffet is always provided with a bar for drinks and a small charge is made to cover costs.

Anyone interested in attending in the future should please look at the club's website for information or make contact through anybody they may know who is already a Diehard.

When asked to recall their outstanding memories of their time with Dartford Harriers, this older group recalled not so much their own or others' athletic performances and achievements, but their deep feelings of having belonged to such a happy and friendly club.

Everyone remembered with fondness the welcome given to them by Harry and Eva May when they first turned up at 'the hut' in Central Park, young and shy, not knowing anyone, and how quickly they were integrated into whatever activity was planned for the coming weeks.

Regular socials and prize-givings were held and the annual club dinner was the highlight of the year.

Outings were arranged to the ice rink and to theatres by the ever-busy Eva May, along with hikes to local beauty spots followed by a drink in a local pub.

New members were encouraged to be as active in the club's social life as they were in their athletic endeavours, and the friendships that developed in the enjoyment of their youthful activities have endured for many years and spawned several long and happy marriages.

Chapter Thirteen

1948 London Olympic Torch Relay

Three Dartford Harriers are known to have taken part in the 1948 London Olympic Torch Relay, namely Alan Dyter, Alf Bennett and Jim Kierans.

Only Alan Dyter was directly representing Dartford Harriers. It seems likely that just one member per club would provide an ample number of bearers. He carried the torch on the Westerham leg of the relay. Alan's brother Frank was club press secretary at the time.

Alf Bennett had been running with Dartford Harriers for many years, gaining his 'Kent representative vest' in 1929. He carried the Olympic torch on the Charing leg of the relay, representing London Paper Mills.

In those days the participants of the relay were allowed to retain the torch they carried. Alf Bennett delighted members by bringing his Olympic torch along to the opening of the Dartford Harriers' new clubhouse in 1997 for others to see. A picture of this is displayed below. Alf's torch has been passed down to his great grandson Tom Goodall, who was until recently an active member of the club.

Alf's sister, Joyce White, recently commented, 'I was so disappointed that I could not see him run in the early hours of that morning, as I had recently given birth to my first child.'

Jim Kierans, a Kent police inspector, was at the time also being asked to compete at national level in middle-distance track races. He actually represented Kent police in the Olympic torch relay.

Arthur Head was another member who was very competitive at that time; he recalls that the club volunteer had to be 'drawn from a hat'. One can imagine what rivalry there must have been for this task! Club membership swelled in 1948 from the normal level of about 100 to nearly 200, which sometimes happens at the time of increased athletic interest surrounding the Olympic Games.

This book is being written at a time when preparations for the 2012 London Olympic Games are in full swing. This is understandably generating considerable media interest and attention, with regular reports on the progress of the Olympic stadium site, all of which are frequently featured on our television screens. This is a far cry from the belated decision to hold the 1948 Olympic Games in London, which by comparison attracted scant attention.

Alf Bennett running his leg of the relay with the 1948 Olympic torch

Alan Dyter running his leg of the relay with the 1948 Olympic torch

Alf Bennett's Olympic torch, given to him after the relay

Appendix A

Club Records

Age groups explained in relation to club records

Children aged under 11 are not recognised by the athletics authorities for competition.

Children aged 11–16 are classified into two year age groups, eg boys aged under 13 = boys aged 11 and 12.

Men and women aged 17–19 are classified into three year age groups, eg women aged under 20 = women aged 17, 18 and 19.

Men and women aged 20–34 are classified as Senior Men and Senior Women.

Athletes over 35 are referred to as Masters and are classified in five year age groups, eg M50 = men aged 50–54.

Club records

BOYS U13

60m	Philip Murphy	9.5	Crawley	23.09.96
75m	Craig Paton	10.5		94
80m	Andrew Webster	10.3	Bromley	19.06.99
100m	Daniel Crawford	12.8	Battersea	17.08.96
	Andrew Webster	12.8	Tonbridge	13.06.99
150m	Robert Browning	20.4		94
200m	Andrew Webster	26.4	Tonbridge	13.06.99
300m	Ian Rumsey	44.9		92
400m	James Cross	59.4	Dartford	28.09.97
600m	Kirk Halliwell	1:43.5		94
800m	James Cross	2:17:1	Kingston	03.08.97
1000m	Tom Fahey	3:10.7	Tonbridge	31.03.97
1500m	Tom Fahey	4:45.4	Woodford	20.07.97
1 mile	Alistair Couling	5:22:7	Dartford	06.08.77
3000m	Steve Wilson	10:13.6	Dartford	08.84
75mH	Lewis Jackson	12.6	Erith	20.09.09
80mH	Justin Lovell	13.6	Dartford	03.07.88
HJ	Tom Morgan	1.61	Deangate	09.02
LJ	Ian Rumsey	4.85	Dartford	29.08.92
TJ	Gary Bignall	10.59		85
PV	Max Hall	2.11	Dartford	02.10.99
DT	Stephen Turner	26.60	Bromley	18.06.95
JT	Timothy Billings	38.36	Dartford	10.04.05
SP	Timothy Billings	8.89	Dartford	25.09.05
Pent	Douglas Brown	1584	Deangate	08.08.93

4x100m	Chris Day, James Chatt Adrian Cooper, Ian Rumsey	53.9		92
4x200m	Chris Day, James Chatt Adrian Cooper, Ian Rumsey	1:58.4	Croydon	05.07.92
4x400m	Ben Ormsby, James Cross, Lee Campion, Tom Fahey	4:20.6	Ashford	14.09.97
4x800m	Rob Kettle, Steve Wilson, Chris Cotton, Jason Thompson	9:50.9	Bromley	09.83
Medley	Keith Seagers, Stuart Longhurst, Simon Neale, Alistair Couling	4:36.4	Crofton	17.04.77

Club records

BOYS U15

60m 1	Daniel Crawford	7.7	Crystal Palace	20.02.98
80m	Doug Christie	10.4	Havering	03.79
100m	Gavin Comber	11.3	Richmond	08.09.02
150m	Gavin Comber	18.03	Tonbridge	01.04.02
200m	Gavin Comber	23.3	Tonbridge	06.08.02
200m 1	Will Dellow	25.73	Lee Valley	07.02.10
300m	Will Dellow	39.13	Dartford	24.04.10
400m	Darren Pinder	53.2	Crystal Palace	05.07.81
600m	Ian Barham	1:34.4	Crystal Palace	18.03.79
800m	Keith Smith	2:02.3	Crystal Palace	05.07.81
1000m	Keith Smith	2:41.1	Crystal Palace	11.09.81
1500m	Terry Hawkey	4:18.89	Hendon	13.08.98
1 mile	Tom Fahey	4:44.9	Erith	26.09.99
3000m	Rob Kettle	9:17.8	Bromley	21.07.85
60mH 1	Liam Lucas	9.6	Crystal Palace	22.02.97
80mH	Luke Allwright	11.8	Dartford	23.09.07
HJ	John Portway	1.81	Tooting	18.07.93
	Chris Davidson	1.81	Derby	90
	Michael Sampson	1.81	Hornchurch	20.07.86
HJ 1	David Johnson	1.65	Crystal Palace	25.02.95
	Matthew Bennett	1.65	Crystal Palace	25.02.95
LJ	Philip Murphy	6.39	Dartford	24.09.00
LJ 1	Tim Billings	5.73	Carshalton	03.03.07
TJ	Tristan Demuth	12.09	Tonbridge	03.09.06
TJ 1	Max Hall	10.26	Crystal Palace	18.02.01
PV	Max Hall	3.00	Dartford	22.09.01
PV 1	Max Hall	2.50	Crystal Palace	17.02.01
DT	Tim Billings	32.66	Ashford	12.05.07
HT	Jason Barker	40.16	Newham	85
JT	Tim Billings	49.30	Copthall	26.08.07
SP	Tim Billings	13.59	Copthall	26.08.07
SP 1	Tim Billings	11.84	Carshalton	03.03.07
Pent	Adam Chalk	2613	Exeter	15.09.07
Pent 1	Douglas Brown	1643	Crystal Palace	23.01.94
Pent 1 60m	Tom Morgan	2369	Bedford	11.01.04

4x100m	David Middleton, Steve Wild, Keith Franklin, Matthew Love	47.9	Bromley	15.09.85
4x200m	David Bacon, Anthony Lewis	1:44.3	Dartford	06.08.77
	David Leadbetter, Steve Fletcher			
4x400m	David Norris, Chris Wilson	3:43.2	Bromley	26.04.81
	Keith Smith, Darren Pinder			
4x800m	S.Owen, Alistair Couling	9:00.7	Bracknell	06.08.87
	Mark Maton, Wilson McVitie			
Medley	Matthew Love, Keith Franklin, Steve Wild, Rob Kettle	3:50.6		85

Club records

BOYS U17

60m 1	Gavin Comber	7.17	Bedford	17.01.04
80m	Keith Hay	9.6	Tonbridge	28.03.76
	James Chatt	9.6	Crawley	23.03.96
100m	Paul Colwell	10.8	Crystal Palace	18.05.80
150m	Gavin Comber	16.5	Tonbridge	19.04.04
200m	Gavin Comber	21.61	Watford	30.05.04
200m 1	Gavin Comber	22.58	Birmingham	29.03.04
300m	James Chatt	36.0	Tonbridge	02.04.96
400m	Ian Bishop	50.0	Colindale	11.09.79
	James Chatt	50.0	Basildon	16.06.96
600m	Bill Addison	1:24.1		81
800m	Keith Smith	1:54.2	Tonbridge	14.07.82
1000m	Bill Addison	2:34.0		81
1500m	Gary Arthey	4:01.69	Crystal Palace	22.07.01
1 mile	Bill Addison	4:27.0		81
3000m	Tom Fahey	8:39.4	Watford	25.07.01
5000m	Tom Fahey	15:29.2	Richmond	23.06.01
60mH 1	Liam Lucas	8.9	Crystal Palace	05.07.81
100mH	Adam Chalk	13.53	Ashford	23.05.09
200mH	Adam Chalk	28.3	Dartford	28.09.08
300mH	Jon Petts	44.0	Crawley	23.03.96
400mH	Adam Chalk	55.4	Mile End	21.06.09
1500mSC	Andrew Wilson	4:30.0	Crystal Palace	05.07.81
2000mSC	Bill Addison	6:23.0		81
3000mSC	Bill Addison	10:06.0		81

HJ	John Portway	1.97	Dartford	21.05.95
HJ 1	Max Hall	1.86	Chelmsford	17.02.03
LJ	Chris Davidson	6.86	Crystal Palace	05.93
LJ1	Tom Goodall	6.19	Sutton	06.03.05
TJ	Darren Graham	13.30		86
TJ 1	Jack Fox	12.69	Sutton	04.03.07
PV	Max Hall	3.80	Sheffield	17.08.03
PV 1	Max Hall	3.80	Chelmsford	19.04.03
DT	Tim Billings	39.08	Parliament Hill	31.05.09
HT	Russell Bethell	45.41	Dartford	23.09.01
JT	Tim Billings	55.71	Southampton	20.06.09
SP	Tim Billings	15.71	Kingston	27.06.09
SP 1	Max Hall	10.51	Bedford	12.01.03
Pent 1	Adam Chalk	2613	Lee Valley	06.01.08
Pent 1 60m	Tom Goodall	2874	Sutton	08.01.06
Oct	Adam Chalk	4836	Kingston	27/28.06.09
Dec	Max Hall	5357	Birmingham	09/10.09.03

4x100m	Duncan Bennett, David Bacon	45.3	Crystal Palace	30.06.79
	Paul Colwell, Ian Bishop			
4x200m	John Giles, Clive Cook	1:37.2	Dartford	29.07.78
	David Bacon, Ian Bishop			
4x400m	Kevin Marriner, Kevin Growns	3:31.0		
	Jason Thompson, Mark Sampson			
Medley	David Bacon, John Giles	3:47.0	Crystal Palace	16.04.78
	Anthony Lewis, Anthony Marshall			

Club records

Men U20

60m 1	James Chatt	6.9	Crystal Palace	14.01.98
80m	James Chatt	9.4	Crawley	22.03.97
100m	James Chatt	10.67	Bedford	04.07.98
150m	Gavin Comber	16.5	Tonbridge	28.03.05
200m	Gavin Comber	21.55	Crystal Palace	17.06.06
200m 1	James Chatt	21.63	Birmingham	15.02.98
300m	James Chatt	34.6	Tonbridge	13.04.98
400m	Ian Bishop	48.5	Crystal Palace	12.05.80
600m	Doug Ives	1:22.5	Crystal Palace	06.03.77
800m	Rob Kettle	1:52.7	Dartford	11.08.90
800m 1	Bill Addison	1:55.7	Cosford	19.03.82
1000m	Bill Addison	2:29.2	Tonbridge	13.07.83
1500m	Jon Grix	3:50.91	Cleckheaton	07.08.83
1500m 1	Jon Grix	4:01.7	Cosford	19.03.82
1 mile	Geoff Wightman	4:36.6	Dartford	03.06.78
3000m	Rob Kettle	8:20.8	Watford	11.07.90
3000m 1	Jon Grix	8:37.46	Cosford	18.03.83
5000m	Geoff Wightman	14:26.6	Crystal Palace	12.09.79
10000m	Andrew Pickett	33:01.0	Catford	14.06.00
60mH 1	Adam Chalk	8.43	Lee Valley	30.01.10
110mH	Liam Lucas	14.93	Exeter	06.07.01
200mH	Jamey Elliott	29.7	Dartford	28.09.08
300mH	Jon Petts	44.6	Crawley	22.03.97
400mH	Darren Graham	55.3		
2000mSC	Andrew Wilson	6:03.51	Cleckheaton	07.08.83
3000mSC	Derek Wightman	9:44.4	Brighton	07.08.82

HJ	Chris Davidson	2.00	Bedford	03.07.94
HJ 1	Max Hall	1.93	Cardiff	13.03.05
LJ	Chris Davidson	7.46	Bedford	03.07.94
LJ 1	Chris Davidson	7.21	Birmingham	12.02.94
TJ	Roland Walker	13.99	Eltham	15.08.81
TJ 1	Jack Fox	13.45	Lee Valley	27.01.08
PV	Max Hall	4.10	Stoke	31.07.05
PV 1	Max Hall	4.00	Cardiff	12.03.05
DT	Max Hall	36.89	Deangate	24.04.05
HT	Jason Barker	34.30	Crystal Palace	15.05.88
JT	Daniel Shaw	54.70	Kingston	21.06.09
SP	Max Hall	12.30	Southampton	17.09.05
SP 1	Tim Billings	14.15	Lee Valley	17.01.10
Pent 1 60m	Max Hall	2921	Bedford	11.01.04
Hept 1	Max Hall	4806	Cardiff	12/13.03.05
Dec	Max Hall	6556	Stoke	30/31.07.05

4x100m	Trevor Atkins, John Giles Ian Bishop, Paul Colwell	43.6	Crystal Palace	20.04.80
4x200m	Ian Bishop, Jeffrey Champion Trevor Atkins, Paul Colwell	1:33.7	Southend	26.07.80
4x400m	Richard Pooley, Darren Bruce Cliff Lucas, Eddie Nicholson	3:247		88
4x1500m	Derek Wightman, Mark Norman Anthony Marshall, Wilson McVitie	18:13.0	Bracknell	81
Medley	Jeffrey Champion, Graham Dray Peter Champion, Anthony Marshall	3:41.1	Bracknell	13.07.80

Club records

60m 1	James Chatt	6.90	Glasgow	19.02.01
80m	James Chatt	9.2	Crawley	24.03.01
100m	Kevin Marriner	10.5	Crystal Palace	16.05.92
150m	Kevin Marriner	16.2	Havering	15.03.92
	Mike Barrett	16.2		
200m	James Chatt	21.2	Bedford	01.07.01
200m 1	James Chatt	22.25	Birmingham	28.01.01
300m	Kevin Marriner	34.4	Havering	15.03.92
400m	James Chatt	46.82	Birmingham	26.07.03
400m 1	James Chatt	48.50	Cardiff	03.02.02
600m	Jason Thompson	1:19.8	Eltham	20.04.96
800m	Jason Thompson	1:50.1	Watford	14.07.96
800m 1	Rob Kettle	1:50.82	Birmingham	15.02.92
1000m	Jason Thompson	2:25.07	Loughborough	18.05.97
1500m	Geoff Wightman	3:47.2	Crawley	17.09.88
1 mile	Geoff Wightman	4:00.6	Thurrock	09.09.88
3000m	Geoff Wightman	7:59.3	Swindon	10.07.86
3000m 1	Geoff Wightman	8:08.42	Cosford	24.01.87
2 miles	Geoff Wightman	8:40.48	Crystal Palace	17.09.82
5000m	Geoff Wightman	13:42.8	Essen	02.09.88
10000m	Geoff Wightman	29:17.88	Birmingham	23.06.89
60mH 1	James McCafferty	9.4	Crystal Palace	13.12.97
110mH	John Giles	15.2	Brighton	30.04.83
200mH	Lee Capon	32.4	Dartford	28.09.08
300mH	Terry Gibbs	42.5	Crawley	20.03.99
400mH	Steve Munday	54.82	Crystal Palace	26.06.81
3000mSC	Geoff Wightman	8:56.9	Bournemouth	31.08.86

HJ	Peter Champion	1.94	Hornchurch	10.05.81
HJ 1	Max Hall	1.89	Sheffield	14.01.06
LJ	Roland Walker	6.96	Dartford	10.05.87
LJ 1	Max Hall	6.76	Sheffield	14.01.06
TJ	Roland Walker	15.43	Dartford	10.05.87
TJ 1	Alex Lee	11.73	Bedford	17.01.04
PV	Max Hall	4.00	Loughborough	
PV 1	Max Hall	4.03	Sheffield	15.01.06
DT	Malcolm Willden	40.94	Eltham	28.06.80
JT	Max Hall	51.72	Dartford	05.08.06
HT	Keith Robinson	43.66		04
SP	Malcolm Willden	13.01	Bournemouth	06.06.81
SP 1	Max Hall	11.95	Loughborough	16.12.06
Hept	Max Hall	4716	Sheffield	14/15.01.06
Dec	Max Hall	5672	Erith	20/21.09.08

4x100m	Darren Bruce, Sean Reilly Mike Barrett, Kevin Marriner	42.9	Tonbridge	08.09.92
4x200m	Dave Muttett, Colin King Arthur Kimber, Dean Powell	1:38.6	Dartford	06.08.77
4x400m	Jason Thompson, Sean Reilly Kevin Marriner, Darren Bruce	3:17.3	Tonbridge	08.09.92
Medley	Paul Oakes, Dave Kemp Eddie Nicolson, Geoff Wightman	3:29.3	Bromley	18.09.88

Club records

MASTERS M40

Event	Name	Time	Venue	Date
60m	Brian Barker	7.7	Crystal Palace	79
60m 1	Dave Kemp	7.56	Eskilstuna	11.03.05
100m	Dave Kemp	11.72	Battersea	13.06.04
150m	Dave Kemp	17.6	Tonbridge	19.04.04
200m	Dave Kemp	23.87	Battersea	13.06.04
200m 1	Dave Kemp	24.06	Linz	15.03.06
300m	Dave Kemp	39.3	Bromley	03.04.04
400m	Dave Kemp	52.7	Dartford	26.09.04
600m	Arthur Kimber	1:26.9	Battersea	01.08.77
800m	Arthur Kimber	2:00.8	Wolverhampton	26.07.81
1000m	Arthur Kimber	2:34.0	Deangate	15.04.78
1500m	Arthur Kimber	4:05.4	Windsor	04.08.79
1 mile	Tim Orr	4:40.9	Erith	26.09.99
3000m	Arthur Kimber	8:50.5	Havering	16.09.81
5000m	Brian Buonvino	15:09.8	Dartford	.83
10000m	Brian Buonvino	32:22.0	Dartford	18.05.82
60mH 1	Gary Capon	11.7	Eton	18.11.01
110mH	Doug Christie	18.1	Erith	17.09.06
200mH	Doug Christie	32.2	Dartford	23.09.07
300mH	Cab Ellis	46.9	Dartford	23.09.00
400mH	Peter Field	60.3	Cologne	13.09.72
1500mSC	Tim Orr	5:06.2	Kingston	27.06.00
2000m	Tim Orr	7:02.2	Eltham	17.05.99
3000m	Tim Orr	10.23.8	Eltham	31.07.99

HJ	Paul Oakes	1.75	Croydon	06.06.93
HJ 1	Gary Capon	1.55	Eton	02.11.03
LJ	Paul Oakes	6.36	Dartford	31.07.93
LJ 1	Gary Capon	4.84	Eton	02.11.03
TJ	Paul Oakes	12.38	Dartford	31.07.93
PV	Keith Turnbull	3.40	Bromley	.91
DT	Dave Payne	35.50	Dartford	31.03.01
HT	Dave Payne	39.49	Hendon	05.09.99
JT	Keith Turnbull	60.22	Reading	.89
SP	John Fenton	11.49	St. Albans	03.04.97
SP 1	Gary Capon	7.73	Eton	18.11.01
Pent	Paul Oakes	3223	Stoke	08.08.93
Pent 160m	Gary Capon	2429	Eton	02.11.03

Club records

100m	Brian Barker	12.1	Dartford	05.04.81
150m	Dave Muttett	19.9	Tonbridge	13.04.98
200m	Dave Kemp	24.9	Malmo	05.09.08
200m 1	Dave Kemp	24.85	Ancona	27.03.09
300m	Dave Kemp	40.7	Tonbridge	05.05.09
400m	Dave Kemp	56.4	Erith	13.07.09
800m	Arthur Kimber	2:00.85	Strasbourg	16.07.82
800m 1	Arthur Kimber	2:09.2	Cosford	13.03.83
1500m	Arthur Kimber	4:11.35	Strasbourg	14.07.82
1500m 1	Arthur Kimber	4:22.5	Cosford	13.03.83
1 mile	Arthur Kimber	4:36.7	Barnet	14.08.82
3000m	Arthur Kimber	9:03.4	Dartford	21.06.83
5000m	Arthur Kimber	16:30.4	Eltham	03.08.85
10000m	Tony Farmer	35:28.5	Deangate	08.08.93
110mH	Cab Ellis	18.47	Battersea	29.08.04
200mH	George Challand	35.4	Croydon	08.09.91
400mH	Peter Field	62.1		04.09.76
2000mSC	Dave Fisher	8:12.7	Eltham	17.05.99
3000mSC	Tim Orr	11:26.5	Woking	08.07.06
HJ	Gary Capon	1.63	Erith	18.09.05
HJ 1	Gary Capon	1.60	Lee Valley	02.08.09
LJ	Cab Ellis	5.37	Erith	11.07.05
TJ	Cab Ellis	11.05	Bromley	18.07.03
PV	Cab Ellis	3.10	Deangate	09.05.05
DT	Steve Foxon	31.85	Kings Lynn	15.05.99
HT	Steve Harvey	31.57	Dartford	16.05.98
JT	Keith Turnbull	58.14	Colindale	05.09.93
SP	John Fenton	11.57	Perivale	28.06.03

MASTERS M50

Event	Name	Mark	Venue	Date
100m	Dave Muttett	13.1	Catford	04.06.01
150m	Graham Barton	20.5	Dartford	12.09.07
200m	Cab Ellis	26.1	Eltham	27.04.07
400m	Graham Barton	60.3	Dartford	23.09.07
800m	Arthur Kimber	2:18.7	Croydon	08.09.91
1500m	Tony Farmer	4:40.3	Dartford	11.07.97
1 mile	Dave Kitcher	5:23.8	Dartford	14.08.09
3000m	Tony Farmer	10.13.8	Dartford	23.09.00
5000m	Tony Farmer	17.33.0	Dartford	16.07.97
10000m	Tony Farmer	37:20.3	Dartford	11.08.99
100mH	Mike Nunn	22.3	Erith	15.09.01
110mH	Cab Ellis	18.3	Dartford	23.09.07
200mH	Cab Ellis	32.9	Dartford	23.09.07
300mH	Vic Withey	54.2	Dartford	02.10.99
400mH	Peter Field	67.7	Brighton	02.05.81
2000mSC	Vic Withey	8:12.0	Ashford	12.05.01
3000mSC	Tim Orr	11:16.5	Peterborough	19.05.07
HJ	Gary Capon	1.60	Hastings	31.01.10
LJ	Tony Rose	5.20	Erith	20.09.03
TJ	Cab Ellis	10.51	Erith	13.07.07
PV	Cab Ellis	2.90	Erith	13.07.07
DT	Steve Foxon	36.15	Erith	20.09.03
HT	Steve Foxon	32.49	Dartford	23.08.03
JT	John Fenton	45.82	Dartford	28.09.08
SP	John Fenton	12.00	Dartford	28.09.08

Club records

MASTERS M55

100m	Peter Field	13.4	Erith	30.06.87
150m	Mike Nunn	20.8	Dartford	12.09.07
200m	Peter Field	27.1	Dartford	29.08.87
400m	Arthur Kimber	61.3	Deangate	18.09.93
800m	Arthur Kimber	2:18.9	Deangate	18.09.93
800m 1	Arthur Kimber	2:29.02	Glasgow	20.03.94
1500m	Arthur Kimber	4:53.6	Deangate	18.09.93
1 mile	Tony Farmer	5:51.1	Dartford	06.05.04
3000m	Bob Heywood	10:14.2	Worthing	30.06.93
5000m	Bob Heywood	18:46.5	Bromley	21.06.93
10000m	Tony Farmer	41:47.0	Battersea	07.09.05
100mH	Peter Field	19.1	Dartford	19.08.86
1500mSC	Bob Heywood	6:01.3	Worthing	30.06.93
3000mSC	Bob Heywood	12:27.5	Eltham	25.05.93

HJ	Bob Heywood	1.30	Colindale	05.09.93
	Mike Nunn	1.30	Dartford	22.04.05
LJ	Brian Barker	4.75	Bromley	15.06.92
TJ	Brian Barker	8.88	Bromley	15.06.92
DT	Steve Foxon	29.35	Dartford	28.09.08
HT	Keith Robinson	39.52	Erith	13.07.09
JT	John Seeley	23.64	Eltham	27.04.07
SP	Steve Foxon	10.46	Erith	20.09.08

MASTERS M60

100m	Peter Field	13.7	West London	14.08.93
	Mike Nunn	13.7	Erith	17.05.10
150m	Mike Nunn	20.5	Dartford	11.06.10
200m	Mike Nunn	28.1	Erith	20.09.09
300m	Arthur Kimber	45.9	Kingston	14.07.99
400m	Arthur Kimber	63.4	Dartford	28.09.97
400m 1	Arthur Kimber	66.71	Bordeaux	10.03.01
600m	Arthur Kimber	1:49.3	Dartford	14.02.01
800m	Arthur Kimber	2:23.0	Jarrow	31.07.99
800m 1	Arthur Kimber	2:32.94	Bordeaux	11.03.01
1500m	Arthur Kimber	4:50.03	Jarrow	06.08.99
1500m 1	Arthur Kimber	5:12.82	Cardiff	17.02.01
1 mile	Arthur Kimber	5:37.2	Battersea	13.08.97
3000m	Arthur Kimber	11:14.1	Dartford	14.04.99
5000m	Arthur Kimber	19:24.6	Dartford	16.07.97
10000m	Tony Farmer	42:28.0	Battersea	03.09.08
60mH 1	Peter Field	10.7	Birmingham	17.02.95
100mH	Peter Field	17.39	Athens	05.06.94
200mH	Peter Field	33.1	Croydon	08.09.91
300mH	Peter Field	48.27	Turku	27.07.91

HJ	Mike Nunn	1.30	Ashford	06.09.09
LJ	Mike Nunn	4.01	Bromley	07.07.10
TJ	Brian Barker	8.36	Eltham	29.04.96
PV	Peter Field	1.90	Eltham	24.05.93
DT	Alan Champion	25.97	Dartford	24.08.02
HT	Gerald Patrick	22.09	Dartford	26.09.10
JT	Peter Field	27.04	Dartford	28.07.95
SP	Brian Barker	7.93	Eltham	29.04.96

Club records

MASTERS M65

60m 1	Peter Field	9.29	Birmingham	26.02.00
100m	Peter Field	13.94	Exeter	10.08.96
200m	Peter Field	28.64	Exeter	11.08.96
300m	Arthur Kimber	49.8	Tooting	01.06.05
400m	Peter Field	66.7	Exeter	10.08.96
400m 1	Arthur Kimber	67.30	San Sebastian	09.03.03
600m	Arthur Kimber	1:56.4	Battersea	13.07.05
800m	Arthur Kimber	2:30.57	Potsdam	24.08.02
800m 1	Arthur Kimber	2:33.87	Sindelfingen	12.03.04
1500m	Arthur Kimber	5:14.68	Potsdam	19.08.02
1500m 1	Arthur Kimber	5:24.67	San Sebastian	09.03.03
1 mile	Arthur Kimber	5:52.6	Solihull	11.07.04
3000m	Arthur Kimber	11.40.0	Bromley	18.07.03
60mH 1	Peter Field	13.96	Birmingham	28.02.97
100mH	Peter Field	18.13	Cesenatico	10.09.98
300mH	Peter Field	51.22	Malmo	20.07.96
2000mSC	Peter Field	9:29.9	Malmo	26.07.96
HJ	Bob Heywood	1.10	Ashford	07.06.04
LJ	Peter Field	3.94	Eltham	08.06.98
PV	Peter Field	1.40	Eltham	20.05.96
DT	Alan Champion	22.58	Dartford	23.08.03
HT	David Baker	17.83	Erith	30.06.06
JT	Peter Field	23.74	Eltham	29.04.96
SP	David Baker	6.21	Eltham	27.04.07

MASTERS M70

60m 1	Peter Field	9.41	Sindelfingen	10.03.04
100m	Peter Field	15.0	Ladywell	02.06.03
200m	Peter Field	31.4	Erith	23.06.03
	Peter Field	31.4	Dartford	22.04.05
200m 1	Peter Field	31.58	Sindelfingen	10.03.04
400m	Arthur Kimber	72.94	Lahti	04.08.09
400m 1	Arthur Kimber	71.32	Helsinki	23.03.07
800m	Arthur Kimber	2:43.41	Riccione	07.09.07
800m 1	Arthur Kimber	2:47.35	Helsinki	24.03.07
1500m	Arthur Kimber	5:44.75	Birmingham	29.07.07
1500m 1	Arthur Kimber	5:54.75	Helsinki	25.03.07
3000m	Arthur Kimber	12:36.6	Erith	13.07.07
60mH 1	Peter Field	12.24	Cardiff	19.02.05
80mH	Peter Field	15.62	Derby	08.06.03
300mH	Peter Field	54.60	Derby	07.06.03
HJ	Bob Heywood	1.05	Ashford	09.06.08
LJ	Peter Field	3.76	Canterbury	28.07.03
TJ	Arthur Kimber	4.90	Ashford	21.05.07
DT	Bob Heywood	15.60	Bromley	19.06.08
HT	Dave Baker	16.50	Erith	13.07.09
JT	Peter Field	21.96	Erith	06.08.01
SP	Dave Baker	6.33	Eltham	27.04.09

Club records

MASTERS M75

100m	Peter Field	15.3	Ashford	05.06.06
200m	Peter Field	31.53	Poznan	29.07.06
400m	Peter Field	76.0	Erith	30.06.06
80mH	Peter Field	17.18	Poznan	28.07.06
300mH	Peter Field	55.81	Poznan	23.07.06
HJ	Peter Field	1.00	Deangate	12.06.06
JT	Peter Field	16.62	Deangate	12.06.06

MASTER RELAYS – ALL AGES – MEN

4x100m	Graham Barton, Cab Ellis Terry Gibbs, Dave Kemp	48.52	Dartford	30.04.04
4x200m	Graham Barton, Cab Ellis Terry Gibbs, Dave Kemp	1:40.8	Erith	24.05.04
4x400m	Terry Gibbs, Cab Ellis Graham Barton Dave Kemp	3:53.7	Ashford	07.06.04
Medley	Peter Field, Alan Champion Mick O'Donogue, Arthur Kimber	4:20.7	Dartford	30.07.80

GIRLS U13

60M 1	Chloe Hurley-Gale	8.6	Crystal Palace	10.12.99
75m	Chloe Hurley-Gale	10.1	Ashford	16.09.00
80m	Sarah Knowles	11.1	Eltham	13.06.93
	Jessica Whitehorn	11.1	Deangate	22.05.94
100m	Hayley Clements	13.0	Thurrock	20.06.81
150m	Chloe Hurley-Gale	19.9	Dartford	13.09.00
200m	Sarah Harcourt	27.0	Thurrock	19.08.82
	Chloe Hurley-Gale	27.0	Eltham	02.09.00
600m	Lucy Hickmott	1:46.7	Deangate	17.06.07
800m	Alison Mills	2:21.5	Thurrock	19.08.82
1000m	Sophie Corbridge	3:14.04	Deangate	02.05.04
1200m	Sophie Corbridge	3:58.00	Walthamstow	26.06.04
1500m	Phillipa Chapman	4:54.8	Brighton	28.05.88
1 mile	Sophie Corbridge	5:35.5	Dartford	06.05.04
70mH	Alana Watson	11.24	Birmingham	07.09.96
HJ	Kerry Smith	1.51	West London	06.09.80
LJ	Catherine Mooney	4.84	Dartford	16.07.88
DT	Rebecca Saunders	34.80	Ashford	28.08.00
JT	Rachelle Brace	31.34	Dartford	22.09.01
SP	Kate Morris	9.81	Dartford	30.06.95
Pent	Natalie Hickmott	1968	Canterbury	02.07.06
4x100m	Vanessa Mann, Alison Mills Lynne Wilson, Sarah Harcourt	53.5	Bromley	25.05.82
4x200m	Jenny Jenner, Joanne Gibson Hayley Clements, Sarah Harcourt	1:56.3	Dartford	30.05.81
3x800m	Jenny Short, Charlotte Mills Estelle Callow	7:43.6	Barnet	30.06.84

Club records

GIRLS U15

60m 1	Kelly Thomas	8.1	Crystal Palace	26.02.95
80m	Susan McMillan	10.6	Tonbridge	19.03.78
100m	Hayley Clements	11.86	Barnet	02.07.83
150m	Lynn Crowhurst	19.9	Tonbridge	23.02.75
	Anna Wittekind	19.9	Tonbridge	24.03.79
200m	Hayley Clements	24.39	Barnet	02.07.83
200m 1	Natalie Hickmott	26.27	Birmingham	24.02.08
300m	Natalie Hickmott	41.5	Tonbridge	24.03.08
400m	Lucy Hickmott	62.9	Dartford	14.08.09
600m	Sue Elam	1:43.5	West London	04.11.81
800m	Anna Wittekind	2:17.1	Crystal Palace	27.07.79
800m1	Lucy Hickmott	2:28.16	Lee Valley	15.02.09
1000m	Leigh Kettle	3:06.7	Bromley	28.08.89
1200m	Zoe Harris	3:59.6	Havering	15.03.92
1500m	Susan Pendrich	4:37.76	Blackpool	09.07.93
1 mile	Megan Edwards	5:24.7	Dartford	06.05.04
60mH 1	Sam Brown	9.39	Birmingham	23.02.08
75mH	Donna Pert	11.4	Crystal Palace	20.09.80
	Sam Brown	11.40	Ashford	24.05.08
80mH	Kerry Smith	12.3	Haringey	08.08.81
200mH	Natalie Hickmott	33.2	Dartford	28.09.08

HJ	Sharon Heffernan	1.64	Upminster	05.07.80
HJ 1	Faye Riley	1.50	Crystal Palace	11.02.95
	Lauren Vickers	1.50	Carshalton	15.02.04
	Bridie Edwards	1.50	Carshalton	03.03.07
LJ	Sharon Heffernan	5.32	Enfield	22.08.81
LJ 1	Chloe Hurley-Gale	5.04	Crystal Palace	16.02.02
TJ	Megan Edwards	10.10	Dartford	26.09.04
PV	Alex Carlton	2.00	Dartford	23.09.07
DT	Clare Abbott	35.50	Waltham Forest	03.09.88
HT	Fatimah Farag	33.78	Ashford	15.05.05
JT	Rachelle Brace	30.56	Braintree	08.09.02
SP	Zenab Farag	11.43	Crawley	27.08.01
SP 1	Kate Morris	11.14	Crystal Palace	23.02.97
Pent	Lucy Hickmott	2641	Erith	14.09.09
Pent 1 60m	Chloe Hurley-Gale	2715	Bedford	13.01.02
4x100m	Julie McCarthy, Jenny Jenner Hayley Clements, Clare Josey	49.66	Birmingham	16.07.83
4x200m	Jenny Jenner, J. Barnden Sarah Harcourt, Hayley Clements	1:46.8	Bromley	24.07.83
3x800m	Leigh Kettle, Rhonda Munnik Hilary Challand	7:18.4	Bromley	18.09.88
4x800m	Linda Ellis, Claire Holden Tracey Neale, Catherine Grain	10.06.02	Crystal Palace	19.09.76

97

GIRLS U17

60m 1	Kelly Thomas	7.67	Birmingham	15.02.97
80m	Kelly Thomas	10.2	Crawley	22.03.97
100m	Hayley Clements	11.77	Birmingham	27.07.85
	Kelly Thomas	11.77	Sheffield	11.07.97
150m	Gilliam Thornton-Smith	18.8	Tonbridge	19.03.78
200m	Hayley Clements	23.9	Eltham	01.06.85
200m 1	Kelly Thomas	25.70	Birmingham	16.02.97
300m	Natalie Hickmott	39.71	Sheffield	11.07.09
300m 1	Natalie Hickmott	41.25	Lee Valley	06.02.10
400m	Ann Baldock	56.0	West London	19.07.75
400m 1	Natalie Hickmott	59.81	Lee Valley	31.01.10
600m	Rhonda Munnik	1:40.4	Thurrock	07.03.89
800m	Karen Blount	2:16.3	Crystal Palace	06.06.82
800m 1	Nadine Terry	2:23.8	Manchester	17.03.07
1000m	Susan Pendrich	3:05.5	Crawley	26.03.94
1200m	Karen Blount	3:46.9	Havering	24.01.82
1500m	Karen Blount	4:34.6	Tonbridge	14.07.82
1500m 1	Anna Wittekind	4:38.3	Cosford	20.03.82
1 mile	Karen Blount	5:05.3	Barnet	20.08.82
3000m	Amy Smith	9:53.52	Watford	25.07.07
60mH 1	Clare Turner	9.2	Crystal Palace	22.02.97
	Chloe Hurley-Gale	9.2	Carshalton	15.02.04
80mH	Clare Turner	11.72	Sheffield	12.07.96
100mH	Kerry Smith	14.9	Haringey	21.05.83
200mH	Sam Brown	30.2	Dartford	16.07.10
300mH	Sam Brown	44.73	Ashford	12.06.10
400mH	Donna Pert	61.59	Crystal Palace	31.07.82

HJ	Sharon Heffernan	1.70	Haringey	21.05.83
HJ 1	Wendy Palmer	1.63	Cosford	22.03.75
LJ	Kathryn Blackwood	5.74	Southampton	31.05.92
LJ 1	Vicky Lawes	5.21	Crystal Palace	11.02.95
	Chloe Hurley-Gale	5.21	Carshalton	15.02.04
TJ	Megan Edwards	11.53	Dartford	03.09.05
TJ 1	Chloe Hurley-Gale	11.20	Bedford	17.01.04
PV	Sharon Oakes	2.30	Ashford	12.08.97
DT	Rebecca Saunders	41.76	Sheffield	11.07.03
HT	Katy Lamb	41.34	Stevenage	05.09.98
JT	Rachelle Brace	32.53	Bromley	03.04.03
SP	Julie Dunkley	13.46	Croydon	22.06.96
SP 1	Julie Dunkley	12.83	Crystal Palace	25.02.96
Pent	Hayley Barton	2568	Woking	03.08.03
Pent 1	Nadine Terry	2848	Manchester	17.03.017
Pent 160m	Megan Edwards	3012	Sutton	08.01.06
Hept	Megan Edwards	4046	Southampton	17/18.09.05

4x100m	Wendy Palmer, Lesley Dray Ann Baldock, I. Harris	50.0	Crystal Palace	01.06.74
4x200m	Jenny Jenner, Julie McCarthy Andrea Withnall, Hayley Clements	1:42.3	Bromley	16.09.84
4x300m	Hayley Hickmott, Rebecca Francis Amy Williams, Victoria Young	3:22.1	Parliament Hill	23.07.06
4x400m	Megan Edwards, Hayley Hickmott Joanna Coe, Rachelle Ahern	4:11.16	Dartford	05.06.05
3x800m	Karen Blount, Sue Elam Carla Jungreuthmayer	7:03.6	Bromley	23.05.82

Club records

60m 1	Kelly Thomas	7.80	Birmingham	05.02.00
100m	Kelly Thomas	11.93	Watford	02.07.00
150m	Megan Edwards	20.3	Dartford	12.08.07
200m	Hayley Clements	23.8	Bromley	15.06.86
200m 1	Hayley Clements	24.98	Cosford	22.01.88
300m	Grace Clements	43.4	Tonbridge	06.08.02
400m	Donna Pert	57.6	Brighton	11.08.84
400m 1	Elaine Murty	61.93	Dortmund	12.02.06
600m	Elaine Murty	1:40.2	Tonbridge	28.03.05
800m	Rhonda Munnik	2:17.5	Crystal Palace	17.05.92
	Elaine Murty	2:17.5	Eton	16.07.05
800m 1	Elaine Murty	2:18.66	Dortmund	12.02.06
1500m	Rachelle Ward	4:41.1		
1 mile	Rachelle Ward	5:23.7	Dartford	06.05.04
3000m	Rachelle Ward	10:01.5	Oxford	
5000m	Jayne Alexander	20:59.3	Dartford	03.09.03
60mH 1	Chloe Hurley-Gale	9.3	Sutton	06.03.05
100mH	Grace Clements	15.4	Cambridge	17.05.03
200mH	Megan Edwards	31.6	Dartford	23.09.07
400mH	Donna Pert	62.2	Barnet	01.09.84
1500mSC	Grace Clements	6:13.8	Cambridge	25.10.03

HJ	Grace Clements	1.70	Barnet	11.08.01
HJ 1	Grace Clements	1.60	Bedford	19.01.03
LJ	Kathryn Blackwood	5.77	Southampton	04.07.93
LJ 1	Kathryn Blackwood	5.55	Lieven	21.02.93
TJ	Kathryn Blackwood	11.80	Southampton	04.07.93
TJ 1	Kathryn Blackwood	11.28	Birmingham	12.02.94
PV	Grace Clements	2.50	Dartford	24.08.02
DT	Rebecca Saunders	43.41	Erith	25.07.04
	Rebecca Saunders	43.41	Birmingham	09.07.05
HT	Katy Lamb	53.13	Battersea	14.07.01
JT	Grace Clements	32.20	Cambridge	10.11.02
SP	Julie Dunkley	14.36	Bedford	06.07.97
SP 1	Chloe Hurley-Gale	9.33	Sutton	08.01.06
Pent160m	Grace Clements	3161	Bedford	12.01.03
Hept	Grace Clements	4286	Derby	21/22.09.02

4x100m	Kim Taylor, Gemma Robinson Vicky Lawes, Rosie Anderson	51.0	Luton	12.06.94
4x400m	Sarah Simmons, D. Willis Kim Taylor, Alison Martin	4:14.4	Luton	12.06.94

Club records

SENIOR WOMEN

60m 1	Hayley Clements	7.89	Cosford	10.01.88
80m	Susan McNamara	10.3	Tonbridge	23.03.80
100m	Kirstie Taylor	11.8	Colchester	15.07.00
150m	Susan McNamara	18.1	Tonbridge	23.03.80
200m	Ann Baldock	24.4	Woodford	14.08.76
200m 1	Hayley Clements	25.34	Birmingham	26.02.94
300m	Ann Baldock	39.1	Crystal Palace	26.05.76
400m	Hayley Clements	54.62	Crystal Palace	26.06.94
400m 1	Ann Baldock	58.4	Cosford	12.01.79
600m	Anna Wittekind	1:28.1	Loughborough	12.06.83
800m	Anna Wittekind	2:06.5	Stretford	19.07.83
800m 1	Sue Elam	2:14.1	Birmingham	12.03.92
1000m	Anna Wittekind	2:51.7	Motspur Park	09.06.82
1500m	Anna Wittekind	4:18.07	Crystal Palace	15.07.83
1500m 1	Anna Wittekind	4:27.22	Cosford	14.01.84
1 mile	Anna Wittekind	4:50.0	Crystal Palace	01.04.88
3000m	Anna Wittekind	9:19.11	Haringey	18.06.88
3000m 1	Anna Wittekind	9:28.6	Cosford	07.01.84
5000m	Andrea Green	16:27.7	Tonbridge	08.08.00
10000m	Andrea Green	34:39.8	Catford	14.07.00
60mH 1	Grace Clements	8.77	Sheffield	03.02.08
100mH	Grace Clements	14.10	Hengelo	28.06.08
200mH	Claire Capon	31.6	Dartford	23.09.07
300mH	Donna Pert	44.8	Hornchurch	24.03.85
400mH	Donna Pert	59.8	Swindon	04.07.87
2000mSC	Charlotte Burgoyne	8:34.08	Sheffield	
3000mSC	Sarah-Jane Cattermole	12:44.6	Perth, Australia	18.12.04

HJ	Grace Clements	1.81	Birmingham	31.05/01.06.08
HJ 1	Grace Clements	1.78	Sheffield	03.02.08
LJ	Grace Clements	6.00	Delhi	08.10.10
LJ 1	Grace Clements	5.87	Sheffield	03.02.08
TJ	Grace Clements	12.41	Boston, USA	09.04.05
PV	Claire Capon	1.90	Dartford	24.09.06
DT	Clare Abbott	36.82	Crystal Palace	18.05.91
HT	Sarah-Jane Cattermole	40.40	Perth, Australia	23.10.04
JT	Grace Clements	44.32	Desenzano	10.05.09
SP	Grace Clements	13.00	Crystal Palace	15.06.08
SP 1	Grace Clements	12.66	Sheffield	03.02.08
Pent 1	Grace Clements	4237	Sheffield	03.02.08
Pent 160m	Grace Clements	3655	Sutton	08.01.06
Hept	Grace Clements	5819	Delhi	08/09.10.10
Dec	Claire Capon	4425	Oxford	12/13.09.09

4x100m	Jo Heap, Mitch Jones Sarah Simmons, Evette Williams	48.8	Tonbridge	25.05.95
4x200m	Sarah Simmons, Jo Heap Evette Williams, M. Jones	1:43.8	Tonbridge	25.05.95
4x400m	Sue Elam, Donna Pert Helen Gray, Anna Wittekind	3:51.87	Bromley	14.06.87
3x800m	Karen Dyett, Sue Elam Caroline Warren	6:51.8	Barnet	30.06.84
Medley	Megan Edwards, Tracy Cunningham Kirsty Taylor, Elaine Murty	2:53.35	Bedford	18.08.07

Club records

MASTERS W35

60m 1	Kirstie Taylor	8.41	Lee Valley	07.02.10
100m	Pat Oakes	13.4	Watford	03.06.84
150m	Kirstie Taylor	20.09	Tonbridge	05.04.10
150m 1	Pat Oakes	21.8	St. Athans	01.04.84
200m	Pat Oakes	27.4	Bromley	06.05.84
400m	Pat Oakes	65.3	Erith	27.08.84
800m	Cara Oliver	2:22.2	Erith	20.09.08
800m 1	Cara Oliver	2:28.85	Lee Valley	07.02.10
1500m	Cara Oliver	4:51.7	Erith	20.09.08
1500m 1	Cara Oliver	4:54.99	Lee Valley	08.03.09
3000m	Pat Halstead	10:36.6	Southampton	25.06.88
5000m	Cara Oliver	19:46.6	Tonbridge	06.05.08
100mH	Pat Oakes	16.12	Brighton	20.08.84
300mH	Pat Oakes	49.6	Havering	25.03.84
400mH	Pat Oakes	69.1	Crystal Palace	5.09.84

HJ	Pat Oakes	1.54	Brighton	23.08.84
HJ 1	Pat Oakes	1.35	Cosford	13.03.83
LJ	Pat Oakes	5.01	Brighton	23.08.84
LJ 1	Pat Oakes	4.08	Cosford	13.03.83
DT	Tracey Riley	27.14	Battersea	10.06.01
HT	Tracey Riley	23.60	Battersea	10.06.01
JT	Julie Godden	26.44		
SP	Pat Oakes	8.74	Dartford	04.08.81
Pent	Pat Oakes	3291	Brighton	23.08.84
Hept	Pat Oakes	4029	Croydon	28.04.84

MASTERS W40

60m 1	Anne Goad	8.6	Eton	18.11.01
80m	Anne Goad	11.4	Crawley	23.03.02
100m	Pat Oakes	13.7	Dartford	07.08.88
	Anne Goad	13.7	Erith	06.08.01
150m	Donna Brown	22.0	Tonbridge	24.03.08
200m	Pat Oakes	28.7	Colindale	14.06.87
400m	Pat Oakes	66.1	Reading	31.07.88
800m	Stephanie Wood	2:53.8	Bromley	08.06.07
1500m	Jenny Worthington	5:38.2	Deangate	31.05.96
3000m	Maureen Farmer	11:44.0	Oxford	07.91
5000m	Stephanie Wood	20:49.75	Tonbridge	05.05.09
60mH 1	Anne Goad	11.1	Crystal Palace	03.02.02
80mH	Pat Oakes	13.5	Bromley	10.06.87
100mH	Pat Oakes	17.4	Windsor	29.05.87
400mH	Pat Oakes	74.6	Dartford	03.09.88
HJ	Pat Oakes	1.42	Crystal Palace	04.05.86
HJ 1	Anne Goad	1.26	Eton	18.11.01
LJ	Anne Goad	4.58	Battersea	10.06.01
LJ 1	Anne Goad	4.31	Crystal Palace	03.02.02
TJ	Pat Oakes	9.13	Millfield	13.08.89
PV	Anne Goad	2.60	Erith	15.09.01
PV 1	Anne Goad	2.30	Bordeaux	11.03.01
DT	Anne Goad	21.64	Dartford	02.10.99
HT	Jacqui Baker	28.73	Dartford	11.06.99
JT	Anne Goad	28.75	Derby	22.09.01
SP	Sandra Campbell	8.40	Stoke	19.04.09
SP 1	Sandra Campbell	8.90	Lee Valley	22.02.09
Pent 1	Anne Goad	3224	Eton	18.11.01
Hept	Pat Oakes	4057	Bromley	04/05.05.86

Club records

60m 1	Anne Goad	8.66	Sindelfingen	10.03.04
100m	Anne Goad	13.85	Kortrijk	19.06.04
150m	Anne Goad	23.1	Bromley	03.04.04
200m	Teresa May	29.5	Dartford	22.04.05
200m 1	Teresa May	29.6	Cardiff	19.02.05
300m	Teresa May	46.8	Tonbridge	05
400m	Teresa May	71.4	Deangate	09.05.05
800m	Kay Koppel	2:32.0	Brighton	03.08.84
800m 1	Kay Koppel	2:38.3	Cosford	13.03.83
1500m	Kay Koppel	5:15.42	Brighton	21.08.84
1500m 1	Kay Koppel	5:25.5	Cosford	13.03.83
1 mile	Gill Skellon	6:42.1	Dartford	19.06.09
3000m	Kay Koppel	11:36.5	Reigate	19.06.82
5000m	Pat Halstead	21:15.77	Battersea	09.06.02
10000m	Pat Halstead	44:11.0	Erith	19.06.02
60mH 1	Pat Oakes	10.6	Crystal Palace	13.03.94
80mH	Pat Oakes	14.5	Reading	26.09.93
100mH	Pat Oakes	21.1	Dartford	05.09.92
200mH	Teresa Eades	38.7	Dartford	28.029.08
300mH	Pat Oakes	51.8	Dartford	28.08.93
400mH	Teresa May	78.0	Eastbourne	30.04.05

HJ	Teresa May	1.40	Croydon	08.08.04
HJ 1	Teresa May	1.45	Cardiff	19.02.05
LJ	Anne Goad	4.56	Eastbourne	06.09.03
LJ 1	Anne Goad	4.34	Sindelfingen	10.03.04
TJ	Pat Oakes	10.18	Dartford	20.08.94
TJ 1	Pat Oakes	9.70	Crystal Palace	25.02.95
PV	Anne Goad	2.40	Crawley	25.04.04
PV 1	Teresa May	2.10	Cardiff	19.02.05
DT	Anne Goad	25.54	Battersea	13.06.04
HT	Anne Goad	28.27	Dartford	23.09.07
JT	Anne Goad	28.27	Deangate	04.07.08
	Anne Goad	28.27	Birmingham	04.07.08
SP	Anne Goad	9.47	Battersea	13.06.04
SP 1	Anne Goad	8.67	Sindelfingen	10.03.04
Pent 1	Teresa May	3107	Cardiff	23.01.05
Hept	Anne Goad	3940	Sheffield	13/14.09.03
Dec	Anne Goad	5748	Sheffield	11/12.09.04

Club records

MASTERS W50

60m 1	Anne Goad	9.59	Lee Valley	07.03.09
80m	Pat Oakes	12.2	Oxford	07.07.96
100m	Pat Oakes	15.2	Bromley	24.06.96
150m	Teresa Eades	23.44	Tonbridge	13.04.09
200m	Teresa Eades	32.2	Eltham	27.04.09
200m 1	Rosemary Champion	35.25	Cardiff	18.02.01
300m	Rosemary Champion	54.6	Sutton	21.09.97
400m	Pat Halstead	76.6	Dartford	26.09.04
800m	Pat Halstead	2:45.96	Birmingham	27.06.04
800m 1	Pat Halstead	2:55.18	Cardiff	19.02.04
1000m	Pat Halstead	3:39.7	Tonbridge	12.04.04
1500m	Pat Halstead	5:26.9	Birmingham	26.06.04
1500m 1	Pat Halstead	5:26.48	Cardiff	21.02.04
1 mile	Pat Halstead	6:16.0	Dartford	06.05.04
3000m	Pat Halstead	11:55.6	Erith	30.06.06
5000m	Pat Halstead	20:07.79	Ashford	14.05.06
10000m	Pat Halstead	45:40.5	Dartford	16.06.04
80mH	Pat Oakes	14.59	Exeter	11.08.96
200mH	Pat Oakes	39.1	Crawley	02.07.96
300mH	Teresa Eades	61.7	Erith	19.09.09
HJ	Christine Clements	1.35	Dartford	24.08.03
HJ 1	Teresa Eades	1.33	Lee Valley	07.03.09
LJ	Pat Oakes	4.05	Dartford	12.07.96
	Anne Goad	4.05	Kingston	14.06.09
TJ	Pat Oakes	9.39	Malmo	25.07.96
TJ 1	Pat Oakes	9.13	Crystal Palace	07.12.96
PV	Teresa Eades	2.20	Kingston	14.06.09
PV 1	Teresa Eades	2.10	Lee Valley	07.03.09
DT	Anne Goad	25.65	Erith	19.09.10
HT	Anne Goad	26.50	Dartford	26.09.10
JT	Anne Goad	28.14	Ashford	05.09.10
SP	Anne Goad	9.97	Eltham	27.04.09
SP 1	Anne Goad	10.03	Lee Valley	22.02.09
Pent 1	Teresa Eades	2729	Lee Valley	08.03.09

MASTERS W55

60m 1	Rosemary Champion	10.1	Crystal Palace	03.02.02
80m	Rosemary Champion	14.0	Watford	10.04.02
100m	Christine Clements	15.7	Bromley	12.06.09
150m	Rosemary Champion	25.9	Tonbridge	01.04.02
200m	Christine Clements	33.6	Ashford	14.06.10
200m 1	Rosemary Champion	37.02	Cardiff	22.02.04
300m	Rosemary Champion	62.3	Watford	10.04.02
400m	Pat Halstead	86.0	Deangate	02.05.08
800m	Pat Halstead	2:57.4	Tonbridge	03.06.08
1500m	Pat Halstead	5:44.33	Riccione	07.03.09
1500m 1	Pat Halstead	5:51.42	Lee Valley	07.03.09
1 mile	Pat Halstead	6:18.0	Dartford	14.08.09
3000m	Pat Halstead	11:58.6	Deangate	02.05.08
5000m	Pat Halstead	21:04.96	Ashford	01.06.08
60mH 1	Christine Clements	12.0	Lee Valley	24.01.10
80mH	Christine Clements	16.3	Erith	19.09.09
HJ	Christine Clements	1.33	Dartford	28.09.08
HJ 1	Christine Clements	1.27	Lee Valley	24.01.10
LJ	Christine Clements	3.96	Ashford	06.09.09
LJ1	Christine Clements	3.46	Lee Valley	24.01.10
TJ	Christine Clements	8.39	Erith	11.07.08
TJ 1	Rosemary Champion	7.47	Sutton	23.03.03
DT	Rosemary Champion	23.87	Dartford	31.03.01
HT	Christine Clements	18.39	Canterbury	18.05.09
JT	Rosemary Champion	19.62	Dartford	30.04.04
SP	Christine Clements	7.42	Erith	19.08.10
SP 1	Christine Clements	7.34	Lee Valley	24.01.10
Pent 1	Christine Clements	3124	Lee Valley	24.01.10

Club records

MASTERS W60

60m 1	Rosemary Champion	10.8	Carshalton	18.02.07
100m	Rosemary Champion	17.5	Erith	20.09.09
150m	Rosemary Champion	28.6	Tonbridge	09.04.07
200m	Kay Koppel	37.3	Dartford	24.09.00
400m	Kay Koppel	92.1	Eltham	19.06.00
	Maureen Farmer	92.1	Ashford	21.05.07
800m	Maureen Farmer	3:34.1	Erith	27.06.08
1500m	Maureen Farmer	6:58.2	Deangate	15.06.07
3000m	Maureen Farmer	14:52.8	Deangate	02.05.08
80mH	Kay Koppel	20.2	Battersea	10.06.01

HJ	Kay Koppel	1.14	Dartford	23.09.00
HJ 1	Kay Koppel	1.10	Crystal Palace	13.02.00
LJ	Kay Koppel	3.36	Ashford	17.09.00
LJ 1	Rosemary Champion	3.10	Carshalton	18.02.07
TJ	Kay Koppel	7.04	Hendon	21.07.99
TJ 1	Kay Koppel	6.79	Eton	04.02.01
DT	Kay Koppel	21.30	Ashford	17.09.00
HT	Rosemary Champion	13.96	Erith	31.07.06
JT	Kay Koppel	16.41	Dartford	24.09.00
SP	Kay Koppel	7.64	Hendon	21.07.99
SP 1	Kay Koppel	7.30	Eton	04.02.01

MASTERS W65

60m 1	Kay Koppel	11.3	Eton	18.11.01
200m	Kay Koppel	38.26	Sheffield	08.09.01
800m	Kay Koppel	3:38.40	Solihull	12.08.01
60mH 1	Kay Koppel	13.8	Eton	18.11.01
80mH	Kay Koppel	18.9	Erith	15.09.01
HJ	Kay Koppel	1.12	Solihull	12.08.01
HJ 1	Kay Koppel	1.05	Eton	18.11.01
LJ	Kay Koppel	3.21	Eton	23.06.01
LJ 1	Kay Koppel	2.90	Eton	18.11.01
TJ	Kay Koppel	6.81	Erith	15.09.01
DT	Kay Koppel	20.24	Copthall	27.07.02
JT	Kay Koppel	17.53	Erith	15.09.01
SP	Kay Koppel	7.60	Eton	23.06.01
SP 1	Kay Koppel	7.33	Eton	18.11.01
Pent	Kay Koppel	3582	Solihull	11.08.01
Pent 1 60m	Kay Koppel	3392	Eton	18.11.01
Hept	Key Koppel	4516	Sheffield	08/09.09.01

MASTERS W70

HT	Val Case	12.83	Erith	15.09.07

MASTERS RELAYS – ALL AGE GROUPS – WOMEN

4x100m	Anne Goad, Gill Skellon Teresa May, Dawn Corbidge	57.8	Dartford	22.04.05
4x200m	Rosemary Champion, Gill Skellon Carol Phillips, Carolyn Watson	2:11.4	Bromley	12.07.99
4x400m	Cara Oliver, Andrea Andrews Gill Skellon, Stephanie Wood	5:10.3	Ashford	29.06.09
Medley	Anne Goad, Teresa May Gill Skellon, Dawn Corbidge	4:53.1	Bromley	11.09.05

Club records

ALL-AGE RECORDS – STANDARD EVENTS

MEN

100m	Kevin Marriner	10.5	1992	93.90
200m	James Chatt	21.2	2001	93.02
400m	James Chatt	46.82	2003	92.46
800m	Jason Thompson	1:50.1	1996	91.48
1500m	Geoff Wightman	3:47.2	1988	91.41
5000m	Geoff Wightman	13:42.8	1988	94.60
10000m	Geoff Wightman	29:17.88	1989	92.06
Mar	Geoff Wightman	2:13.17	1991	94.59
110mH	John Giles	15.2	1983	84.93
400mH	Steve Munday	54.82	1981	85.33
3000mSC	Geoff Wightman	8:56.9	1986	89.92
HJ	Chris Davidson	2.00	1994	81.96
LJ	Chris Davidson	7.46	1994	86.24
TJ	Roland Walker	15.43	1987	85.86
PV	Max Hall	4.10	2005	70.32
DT	Malcolm Willden	40.94	1980	56.43
HT	Keith Robinson	43.66	2004	69.42
JT	Keith Turnbull	60.22	1989	75.67
SP	Malcolm Willden	13.01	1981	58.60
Dec	Max Hall	5672	2008	

WOMEN

100m	Hayley Clements	11.77	1985	93.79
	Kelly Thomas	11.77	1997	93.79
200m	Hayley Clements	23.8	1986	91.51
400m	Hayley Clements	54.62	1994	87.69
800m	Anna Wittekind	2:06.5	1983	89.23
1500m	Anna Wittekind	4:18.07	1983	89.30
5000m	Andrea Green	16:27.7	2000	87.46
10000m	Andrea Green	34:39.8	2000	86.31
Mar	Sarah Rowell	2:28.06	1985	93.88
100mH	Grace Clements	14.10	2008	86.59
400mH	Donna Pert	59.8	1987	88.19
HJ	Grace Clements	1.81	2008	86.60
LJ	Grace Clements	5.87	2008	78.05
TJ	Grace Clements	12.41	2005	82.12
PV	Anne Goad	2.60	2001	71.82
DT	Rebecca Saunders	43.41	2004	64.26
HT	Katy Lamb	53.13	2001	93.16
JT	Grace Clements	44.32	2009	55.40
SP	Julie Dunkley	14.36	1997	69.91
Hept	Grace Clements	5740	2009	

The figures on the right hand side of the list are age graded scores out of 100.

ROAD RUNNING – MEN

U20

10K	Richard Pooley	32:58	Brands Hatch	85
10M	Andrew Pickett	58:44	Sittingbourne	06.10.02

SM

10K	Geoff Wightman	29:23	Hemel Hempstead	04.04.87
10M	Geoff Wightman	47:54	Bradford	24.08.87
½Mar	Geoff Wightman	63.03	The Hague	05.04.86
25K	Ian Patten	1:16:39		87
20M	David Powell	1:47:16	Worthing	86
Mar	Geoff Wightman	2:13:17	Berlin	29.09.91
40M	Mark Guichard	4:21:30		85
50M	Mark Guichard	5:35:35		85
100K	Mark Guichard	8:28:25		84
100M	Alan Munday	16:33:13		84
24hours	Alan Munday	133M 621Y		84

M40

5K	Tony Durey	18:28	Danson Park	14.03.08
5M	Tony Durey	30:35	Eltham	10.06.07
10K	Roger Friend	32:58		88
10M	Brian Buonvino	51:04		85
½Mar	Brian Buonvino	70:31		82
25K	Roger Friend	1:24:34		88
20M	Brian Buonvino	1:49:03		81
Mar	Barry Nash	2:25.37	London	83
40M	Merv Nutburn	4:59:29		91
50M	Alan Munday	6:18:44		89
100K	Alan Munday	8:55:42		88
100M	John Fitton	20:38:32		83
24hours	John Fitton	113M 1750Y		83

M45

5K	Tony Durey	18:20	Rye	18.09.09
5M	Tony Durey	30:01	Harvel	06.06.09
10K	Brian Buonvino	31:55		86
10M	Brian Buonvino	51:52		85
½Mar	Brian Buonvino	70:37		85
25K	Mike Burgoyne	1:32:19		89
20M	Brian Buonvino	1:52:12		85
Mar	Mike Burgoyne	2:39:32	London	23.04.89
40M	Malcolm Waddell	4:42:42		81
50M	Graham Ives	7:05:02		88
100K	Graham Ives	9:18:04		88

M50

5K	Dave Kitcher	18:05	Battersea	28.07.09
5M	Dave Kitcher	29:25	Harvel	06.06.09
10K	Tony Farmer	36:15	Cliffe	20.06.97
10M	Tony Farmer	61:08	Sittingbourne	10.97
½Mar	Tony Farmer	79:28	Newcastle	10.97
25K	Malcolm Waddell	1:41:15		84
20M	Dave Kitcher	2:10:39	Thanet	02.03.08
Mar	Derek Munday	2:53:47		83
40M	Malcolm Waddell	4:58:57		83
50M	Peter Sargeant	7:02:40		84
100K	Peter Sargeant	9:15:10		84
100M	Peter Sargeant	19:02:22		85
24hours	Peter Sargeant	123M 1419Y		85

Club records

ROAD RUNNING – MEN (cont.)

M60

5k	Tony Farmer	20.54	Danson Park	12.10.07
5M	Tony Farmer	34.54	London	11.08
10K	Bob Heywood	39.47	Beckenham	02.05.97
10M	Bob Heywood	67:37		28.09.97
½Mar	Bob Heywood	1:29.30		
20M	Bob Heywood	2:30:12	Finchley	16.03.97

M65

5K	Arthur Kimber	21:32	Deal	02.01.06
5M	Arthur Kimber	35:16	Witham	26.12.04
10K	Arthur Kimber	42:57	Beckenham	06.05.02

M70

5K	Arthur Kimber	22:37	Deal	01.01.08
10K	Arthur Kimber	46:21	Beckenham	07.05.07

ROAD RUNNING – WOMEN

U17

10K	Amy Smith	36:17	Wilmington	28.10.07

U20

10K	Elaine Murty	40:40	Wilmington	29.10.07

SW

5K	Nicola Thompson	18:17	Stevenage	30.05.99
5M	Sarah Rowell	26:49	Southwark	01.07.84
10K	Sarah Rowell	33:34	Oldham	15.09.85
10M	Sarah Rowell	53:44	Tonbridge	10.03.84
½Mar	Sarah Rowell	72:06	Brighton	11.11.84
20M	Sarah Rowell	1:56:01	Wimbledon	20.07.85
Mar	Sarah Rowell	2:28:06	London	21.04.85

W35

1M	Cara Oliver	5:20	Gillingham	27.07.08
5K	Cara Oliver	19:45	Greenwich	03.07.08
5M	Pat Halstead	31:41	Pitsea	06.11.88
10K	Pat Halstead	39:18	Joydens Wood	11.06.89
10M	Pat Halstead	66.11	Woking	26.02.89
½Mar	Pat Halstead	84:15	Hempstead Valley	29.04.89
Mar	Sheila Cousins	3:21.0	Luton	

W40

5K	Maureen Farmer	22:09	Harrow	09.91
5M	Stephanie Wood	34:28	Harvel	06.06.09
10K	Sue Martin-Clarke	38:31	Lordswood	30.06.96
10M	Sue Martin-Clarke	63:44	Sidcup	15.02.98
½Mar	Sue Martin-Clarke	83:57	Hempstead Valley	05.05.96
25K	Maureen Farmer	2:01:42	Mitcham	01.91
15M	Maureen Farmer	2:26:31	Benfleet	
20M	Sue Martin-Clarke	2:10:28	Worthing	24.03.96
Mar	Sue Martin-Clarke	2:56:59	London	13.04.97

Club records

W45

5K	Gill Skellon	24:26	Rye	20.09.09
5M	Sue Wallace	36:50	Pitsea	12.11.95
10K	Sue Martin-Clarke	41:04	Ashford	08.10.00
10M	Sue Martin-Clarke	65:11	Sidcup	18.02.01
½Mar	Sue Martin-Clarke	87:52	Brighton	25.02.01
20M	Sue Martin-Clarke	2:19:35	Worthing	25.03.01
Mar	Sue Martin-Clarke	3:13:02	Benidorm	26.11.00

W50

10K	Audrey Dyett	45:52	Joydens Wood	11.06.95
10M	Pat Halstead	74:45	Bishops Stortford	20.11.05
½Mar	Audrey Dyett	1:40:55	Maidstone	26.09.99
20M	Audrey Dyett	2:37:24	Thanet	02.03.95
Mar	Audrey Dyett	3:30:08	London	02.04.95

W55

10K	Audrey Dyett	47:04	Cliffe	09.07.00
10M	Audrey Dyett	75:01	Sidcup	20.02.00
½Mar	Audrey Dyett	1:37:52	Paddock Wood	26.03.00
20M	Audrey Dyett	2:40:57	Thanet	05.03.00
Mar	Audrey Dyett	3:35:49	London	16.04.00

W60

5K	Maureen Farmer	25:53	Danson Park	11.05.07
10K	Maureen Farmer	53:55	Brighton	18.11.07
10M	Maureen Farmer	1:29:49	Sittingbourne	07.10.07
½Mar	Maureen Farmer	1:59:44	Palma	21.10.07

RACE WALKING – ROAD – MEN

U13

1K	Jack Tomlin	6:30	Monks Hill	05.12.99
2K	Jack Tomlin	12:25	Birkenhead	06.11.99
2.5K	Jack Tomlin	15:14	Bexley	10.02.01

U15

2K	Jack Tomlin	9:27	Dublin	13.07.03
2.5K	Jack Tomlin	12:40	Victoria Park	02.02.03

U17

3K	Jack Tomlin	24:52	Bexley	14.02.04
10K	Jack Tomlin	52:24	Leamington Spa	04.05

U20

10K	Jack Tomlin	53:48	Leamington Spa	17.06.06

RACE WALKING – TRACK – MEN

U13

1K	Jack Tomlin	6:10.1	Dartford	24.09.00
2K	Jack Tomlin	12:17.9	Wirral	04.11.00
2.5K	Jack Tomlin	15:42.2	Ashford	17.05.01
3K	Matthew Harris	20:40.4	Hull	08.04.01

U15

2K	Richard Harris	10:54.0	Coventry	12.07.01
3K	Jack Tomlin	14:55.3	Sheffield	20.09.03

U17

5K	Jack Tomlin	14.45	Birmingham	29.02.04

Club records

U20

2K	Jack Tomlin	9:23.4	Ashford	10.06.06
3K	Jack Tomlin	14:33.94	Ashford	13.05.06

M40

2K	Graham Cousins	11:10.3	Dartford	25.07.94

M45

2K	Vic Withey	10:20.0	Catford	05.07.99

M50

2K	Vic Withey	10:30.4	Deangate	21:07.00

M55

2K	Mike Burgoyne	12:21.3	Deangate	30.04.99

M60

2K	Bob Heywood	12:31.2	Eltham	28.04.97

M65

2K	Bob Heywood	14:35.2	Eltham	10.05.04

RACE WALKING – ROAD – WOMEN

U13

1K	Carley Tomlin	5:24	Dublin	11.09.99
2K	Carley Tomlin	10:53	Dartford	06.05.00
2.5K	Natasha Fox	13:37	Bexley	12.10.98

U15

2K	Natasha Fox	10:30	Sheffield	24.04.99
2.5K	Nicola Phillips	13:18	Bexley	08.02.97
3K	Nicola Phillips	15:20	Sheffield	26.04.97

U17

3K	Becky Tisshaw	14:39	Dublin	28.09.96
5K	Becky Tisshaw	25:01	Bexley	07.12.96
10K	Nicola Phillips	52:30	Leicester	17.04.99

U20

3K	Becky Tisshaw	15:26	Dublin	27.09.97
5K	Nicola Phillips	25:33	Monks Hill	22.01.00
10K	Nicola Phillips	51:36	Leamington	23.04.00
7M	Nicola Phillips	60:14	Wimbledon	27.11.99
15K	Clare Reeves	82:20	East Molesey	02.03.02
20K	Sarah Foster	1:56:51	East Molesey	25.03.06

SW

5K	Sarah-Jane Cattermole	26:16	Stockport	05.06.99
10K	Sarah-Jane Cattermole	47:04	Australia	07.01
20K	Sarah-Jane Cattermole	1:41:04	Murdoch, Australia	30.11.03

W35

3K	Carolyn Watson	17:45	Woodford	16.09.98
5K	Carolyn Watson	27:56	Bexley	12.02.00
10K	Carolyn Watson	60:14	Surrey	09.01.00

Club records

W40

3K	Elizabeth Harris	23:45	Leamington	04.03.01
5K	Elizabeth Harris	38:24	Hackney	25.03.01

RACE WALKING – TRACK– WOMEN

U13

1K	Natasha Fox	5:14.6	Deangate	31.08.98
1.2K	Carley Tomlin	6:29.3	Battersea	27.05.00
2K	Natasha Fox	11:08.8	Derby	31.05.98
2.5K	Charlotte Curtis	15:14.7	Ashford	09.05.98
3K	Natasha Fox	17:21.0	Woodford	25.07.98

U15

1.6K	Nicola Phillips	7:51.2	Battersea	24.05.97
2K	Nicola Phillips	10:04.7	Bromley	10.08.97
2.5K	Nicola Phillips	12:58.9	Crystal Palace	10.05.97
3K	Sarah Foster	15:12.7	Sheffield	20.09.03
5K	Sarah Forester	28:02.0	Wood Green	27.08.03

U17

2K	Becky Tisshaw	9:27.0	Bromley	10.08.97
2.5K	Becky Tisshaw	12:05.0	Deangate	04.06.97
3K	Becky Tisshaw	14:24.0	Dublin	19.07.97
3K 1	Becky Tisshaw	14:51.86	Chemnitz	01.03.97
5K	Nicola Phillips	25:11.46	Birmingham	21.08.99

U20

2K	Nicola Phillips	10:00.7	Dartford	03.10.99
3K	Nicola Phillips	15:39.86	Crystal Palace	13.05.00
3K 1	Nicola Phillips	14:38.22	Birmingham	06.02.00
5K	Nicola Phillips	27:13.2	Birmingham	16.09.00

SW

1M	Sarah-Jane Cattermole	7:18.04	Perth, Australia	04.12.03
2K	Sarah-Jane Cattermole	9:11.5	Erith	07.05.00
3K	Sarah-Jane Cattermole	14:00.8	Tonbridge	01.04.02
5K	Sarah-Jane Cattermole	24:23.0	Stenning	10.06.01

W35

2K	Carolyn Watson	10:36.5	Bromley	17.04.00
3K	Carolyn Watson	16:32.16	Crystal Palace	14.05.00
3K 1	Carolyn Watson	16:10.3	Birmingham	26.02.00
5K	Carolyn Watson	30:42.82	Gateshead	06.08.99

W40

2K	Kandis Fox	12:51.2	Dartford	03.10.99

W45

2K	Chris Childs	13:06.06	Deangate	02.05.08

W50

2K	Lynne Mallory	13:35.8	Dartford	03.10.99

W55

2K	Christine Clements	14:37.6	Erith	13.07.09

W70

2K	Val Case	17:54.8	Erith	11.07.08

Sullivan Western Challenge Cup for the Best Male Athlete of the Year

Year	Name	Year	Name
1944	Clarrie Dockerill	1978	Arthur Kimber
1945	George Gosling	1979	Gary Huckwell/
1946	Martin Whenman		Geoff Wightman
1947	Roy Johnstone	1980	Gary Huckwell
1948	Martin Whenman	1981	Geoff Wightman
1949	Ray Springate	1982	John Grix/
1950	Den Booker		Keith Smith
1951	Den Booker	1983	Barry Nash
1952	Keith Batchelor	1984	Steve Wilson
1953	Charlie Childs	1985	Michael Witmond
1954	Alan Riddington	1986	John Campbell
1955	David Stevens	1987	Ian Patten
1956	Harry Batten/	1988	Geoff Wightman
	Frank Dyter	1989	Geoff Wightman
1957	Jim Simmons	1990	Geoff Wightman
1958	John Morrison	1991	No award
1959	Malcolm Still	1992	No award
1960	Malcolm Still	1993	No award
1961	Charlie Childs	1994	No award
1962	Colin Ridley	1995	No award
1963	Malcolm Still	1996	No award
1964	Colin Ridley	1997	No award
1965	Colin Ridley	1998	James Chatt
1966	Colin Ridley	1999	Tom Fahey
1967	Colin Ridley	2000	Liam Lucas
1968	Peter Buss	2001	James Chatt
1969	Keith Marshall	2002	Gavin Comber
1970	Paul Toone	2003	James Chatt
1971	John Cassell	2004	Gavin Comber
1972	Michael Dixon	2005	Max Hall
1973	Peter Field	2006	Peter Field
1974	John Cassell	2007	Arthur Kimber
1975	Geoff Wightman	2008	No award
1976	Barry Nash	2009	Adam Chalk
1977	Doug Ives/ Barry Nash		

Mrs Sullivan Challenge Cup for the Best Female Athlete of the Year

1945	Jenny Bond	1978	Donna Goble
1946	Betty Edwards	1979	Anna Wittekind
1947	Betty Edwards	1980	Donna Pert
1948	Brenda McFall	1981	Donna Pert
1949	Eileen Shepherd	1982	Donna Pert
1950	June Lock	1983	Hayley Clements
1951	Rachel Grindell	1984	Sarah Rowell
1952	Rachel Grindell	1985	Sarah Rowell
1953	Joyce Thompson	1986	Hayley Clements
1954	Molly Baker	1987	Donna Pert
1955	Molly Baker	1988	Anna Wittekind/ Leigh Kettle
1956	Doris Batchelor	1989	Michelle Jones/ Rosie Anderson
1957	Doris Batchelor	1990	Claire Heather
1958	Nora Bullen	1991	No award
1959	Molly Titshall (née Baker)	1992	No award
1960	Pamela Hollingham	1993	No award
1961	Janice Eyles	1994	No award
1962	Maureen Conlan	1995	No award
1963	Maureen Conlan	1996	No award
1964	Maureen Conlan	1997	No award
1965	Maureen Conlan	1998	Katy Lamb
1966	Maureen Conlan	1999	Nicola Phillips
1967	Sarah Halliford	2000	Andrea Green
1968	Susan Fickey	2001	Katy Lamb
1969	Jenny Farr	2002	Megan Edwards
1970	Gwen Tume	2003	Rebecca Saunders
1971	Jenny Farr	2004	Chloe Hurley-Gale
1972	Ann Baldock	2005	Megan Edwards
1973	Ann Baldock	2006	Grace Clements
1974	Lynn Crowhurst	2007	Grace Clements
1975	Ann Baldock	2008	Grace Clements
1976	Ann Baldock	2009	Grace Clements
1977	Ann Baldock/ Gilllian Smith		

1991–1997

After contacting and speaking to many members and former members, the authors have been unable, through existing records, to discover any evidence of awards and certainly no names on the trophies in these years. This was a period of some difficulty for the club after the members had to leave the old hut accommodation and relocate in the Bowls Club building. This was subsequently burned down by vandals, forcing members to have to change in a portacabin until the new clubhouse became available.

Dartford Harriers' Officers

Date	President	Chairman	Secretary	Treasurer
1922			W J Western	
1923	Major J C Beadle		W J Western	
1924		H Dutton	W J Western	
1925	Rev Canon L Savill	F G Griffin	W J Western	
1926	Rev L D Hammond	F G Griffin	W J Western	S G E Allnutt
1927	J E Mockridge	F G Griffin	W J Western	S G E Allnutt
1928	A M Fleet JP	F G Griffin	W J Western	C H Selves
1929	A M Fleet JP	F G Griffin	W J Western	C H Selves
1930	A M Fleet JP	F G Griffin	G E Foster	H T Foster
1931	A M Fleet JP	W J Western	G E Foster	H T Foster
1932	A M Fleet JP	W J Western	G E Foster	H T Foster
1933	A M Fleet JP		G E Foster	W J Western
1934	A M Fleet JP		G E Foster	W J Western
1935	A M Fleet JP		G E Foster	W J Western
1936	A M Fleet JP		G E Foster	W J Western
1937	A M Fleet JP	W J Western	G E Foster	W J Western
1938	A M Fleet JP	G H Wolfe	G E Foster	A W Edmonds
1939	A M Fleet JP	G H Wolfe	G E Foster	A W Edmonds
1940				
1941				
1942				
1943	Miss E M Fleet		A E Board	
1944	Miss E M Fleet		A E Board	
1945		E J Hobbs	A E Board	W J Western

1946		E J Hobbs	A E Board	A W Edmonds
1947	Miss E M Fleet	E J Hobbs	A Hope	A W Edmonds
1948	Miss E M Fleet	W J Western	A Dyter/ G Livesley	A W Edmonds
1949	Miss E M Fleet	W Lowe	P Marley	A W Edmonds
1950	Miss E M Fleet	None elected	W J Western	A W Edmonds
1951	W J Western	P Marley	W J Western	A W Edmonds
1952	W J Western	P Marley	W J Western	A E Edmonds
1953	E J Hobbs	P Marley	W J Western	A E Edmonds
1954	A W Edmonds	M S Terry	W J Western	A E Edmonds
1955	P H Selves	A Head	L Hull	W J Western
1956	A F Taylor	A Head	L Hull	W J Western
1957	A F Taylor	J Boland	L Hull	W J Western
1958	A F Taylor	J Boland		W J Western
1959	A F Taylor	J Boland	P E Field	W J Western
1960	A F Taylor	J Boland	P E Field	W J Western
1961	A F Taylor	M Mason	P E Field	J Morrison
1962	A F Taylor	M Mason	P E Field	Mrs A M James
1963	A F Taylor	M Mason	P E Field	Mrs A M James
1964	A F Taylor	M Mason	A M James	Mrs A M James
1965	A F Taylor	M Mason	A M James	P E Field
1966	A F Taylor	M Mason	A M James	P E Field
1967	H and E May	M Mason	A M James	P E Field
1968	J Booker	M Mason	R H Drew	P E Field
1969	Mr and Mrs A M James	M Mason	M Hodder	P E Field
1970	P E Field	M Mason	G Hodder	P E Field
1971	W J Western	M Mason	G Hodder	P E Field
1972	Mrs M Hodder	A Head	G Hodder	P E Field

Year				
1973	L Davis	A Head	G Hodder	P E Field
1974	C Clarke	A Head	G Hodder	P E Field
1975	C Clarke	A Head	G Hodder	P E Field
1976	C Clarke	A Head	A Hill	P E Field
1977	C Clarke	A Head	A Hill	P E Field
1978				P E Field
1979			B Fagg	P E Field
1980			R H Drew	A Hill
1981			R H Drew	A Hill
1982	Mrs N Wightman		R H Drew	A Hill
1983	Mrs N Wightman		R H Drew	A Hill
1984	Mrs N Wightman		R H Drew	A Hill
1985	Mrs N Wightman		R H Drew	A Hill
1986	Mrs N Wightman		R H Drew	A Hill
1987			R H Drew	A Hill
1988	P E Field		R H Drew	A Hill
1989	B Fagg		R H Drew	J Wightman
1990	B Fagg	E Cotton	R H Drew	C Baker
1991	B Fagg	E Cotton	R H Drew	C Baker
1992	P E Field	P E Field	R H Drew	A Champion
1993	P E Field	P E Field	R H Drew	A Champion
1994	P E Field	P E Field	R H Drew	A Champion
1995	P E Field	P E Field	R H Drew	A Champion
1996	P E Field	P E Field	R H Drew	A Champion
1997	P E Field	P E Field	R H Drew	A Champion
1998	P E Field	R H Drew	M Burgoyne	A Champion
1999	P E Field	R H Drew	M McCafferty	A Champion
2000	A Kimber	R H Drew	D Wightman	A Champion
2001	A Kimber	R H Drew	D Wightman	A Bungay
2002	A Kimber	R H Drew	D Wightman	A Bungay
2003	A Kimber	R H Drew	D Wightman	A Bungay
2004	A Kimber	R H Drew	D Wightman	A Bungay

Dartford Harriers' officers

2005	A Kimber	R H Drew	D Wightman	A Bungay
2006	D Wightman	A Kimber	J Marchant	A Bungay
2007	D Wightman	A Kimber	J Marchant	A Bungay
2008	D Wightman	A Kimber	J Marchant	A Bungay
2009	P E Field	A Kimber	Miss C Capon	A Bungay
2010	A Durey	Miss C Capon	Miss C Oliver	Miss R Ward